Octobre 1789 : les Parisiennes marchent sur Versailles. (Musée Carnavalet - Bulloz)

THE REIGN
OF
WOMEN

IN EIGHTEENTH-CENTURY FRANCE

Madame de Pompadour (Boucher)

THE REIGN OF WOMEN is that rare combination — a thoroughly readable book based on a good amount of solid research. Vera Lee's latest work has popular appeal that is in no way diminished by its very sound scholarship; so that with THE REIGN OF WOMEN, the reader is given "the best of both worlds."

The author writes, "the book is designed neither to convince the twentieth century skeptic of the Enlightenment Frenchwoman's enormous prestige and influence nor to debunk her 'Reign.' It represents a totally unfashionable attempt at objectivity." Using a variety of sources (letters, diaries, novels, plays, census reports and contemporary essays on women), she arrives at a "patch work quilt pattern of equality," with women of different ages and classes enjoying different degrees of power.

The book first examines the hierarchy of eighteenth century French feminine society. The author outlines the social ladder and vividly portrays each "rung," from noblewoman to *grisette,* analyzing the amount of freedom each allowed. She goes on to describe the feminist and antifeminist quarrels of the day, paying special attention to Voltaire and Rousseau. Facets of women's education are covered, as are aspects of women's legal rights (including the *duties* of marriage). Dr. Lee concludes with an assessment of female power in France before, during and after the Revolution.

THE REIGN
OF
WOMEN
IN EIGHTEENTH-CENTURY FRANCE

VERA LEE

SCHENKMAN PUBLISHING COMPANY
CAMBRIDGE, MASSACHUSETTS

A Theatre Loge (Moreau the Younger)

Copyright©1975
Schenkman Publishing Company, Inc.
Cambridge, Massachusetts 02138

Library of Congress Catalog Card Number 75-24555

Pour mon Lucien

ILLUSTRATIONS

CONTENTS

Julie de Lespinasse (Carmontelle)

Preface

"The Reign of Women," "Woman's Emancipation," "The Influence
of Women"—what history of eighteenth-century France does not
contain a chapter proclaiming woman's dazzling rise during the
French Enlightenment? A contemporary reader of these histories
might well wonder how—indeed, whether—such a phenomenon
could have been possible. Undoubtedly, for those women who are
currently demanding equal rights and equal opportunities, such optimistic chapter headings would sound rather simplistic and quaint—a
pat sort of optimism more suited to some archaic plasterboard fairy-
land than to the acid reality of our modern society.

This book is designed neither to convince the twentieth-century
skeptic of the Enlightenment Frenchwoman's enormous prestige and
influence nor to debunk the notion of her "Reign." It represents a
totally unfashionable attempt at objectivity. By examining the eighteenth-century Frenchwoman through several important lenses (for
example, social, pedagogical, judicial and moral) I have tried to
probe and answer fairly questions of her liberty, equality and power.
My hope is that, after putting her image into as clear a focus as
possible, I shall provide modern readers with at least a bit more
perspective on the eternally perplexing subject of women.

For a truly exhaustive study of Enlightenment Frenchwomen ten
times as many pages as these would have been too few. I was tempted, for example, to recount in detail lives of fascinating women or
to analyze some of their works. But in focusing on aspects more
pertinent to my goals many ripe plums were left unplucked. For

related material that I have not treated here I refer interested readers to my bibliography, in particular to the last two sections.

Deep gratitude to Professor Otis E. Fellows of Columbia University for taking precious time away from his important work on Diderot to read this manuscript and to offer me his cogent, invaluable suggestions. To Professor L. W. Minor of S. U. N. Y., Fredonia, for his inspiration, encouragement and advice: all my admiration.

Vera Lee
Wellfleet, Mass.
June, 1975

"Adieu" (Moreau the Younger)

1

The Social Ladder

The eighteenth-century Frenchwoman did not exist. History can only identify her in the plural: in several strata of society, at various stages of her life and of her century, in different regions of the country. And, paradoxically, she was as singular as her fingerprints. If we can rediscover her elusive image today, perhaps the most likely place to begin looking is where she would most like to be found—at the height of her beauty and power, in the flowering of her era and at the top of the creamiest layer of French society—the court nobility.

"A court without women is a year without spring and a spring without roses," said King François I in the sixteenth century, as he enticed baronesses and countesses from their castles into his own exciting entourage. But in the first years of the eighteenth century, the roses were close to withering in the dry and oppressive atmosphere of Versailles, stifled by the fetid breath of an aging, soberly repentant Louis XIV. When the old king died in 1715 and Philippe d'Orléans became regent, mourning was lost in the overwhelming joyous relief. For women as well as men freedom came into style, intellectual liberty stimulating moral license. Then large formal palaces gave way to more livable *hôtels,* the boudoir vied with the salon, furniture became more comfortable, dresses gauzier and more décolleté and songs more risqué. Poetry neglected the sublime for the witty. Painting turned its back on the grand and heroic subjects preferred by the Sun King and charmed viewers instead with feminine grace and gallantry. Watteau had already set the tone with his magical silk-and-satin love scenes under the trees. And the somber, virile tones of seventeenth-century oil painting were fast forgotten in the barrage of delicate pastels introduced in France by the Venetian artist Rosalba Carriera. Miniature portraits enjoyed a vogue—not a surprising fact since all dimensions seemed to have shrunk in the direction of intimacy. As proof of this, *petit* was a favored word in an upper-class woman's vocabulary. She had her informal little rooms in her home or her *petits appartements,* she gave her *petits* suppers and often kept a *petit* hideaway in the country for her *petit* lover.

The aim was no longer to impress but to please and amuse, and it was generally the females who insisted on it. Even celebrated philosophers and scientists wrote tracts to interest women who were curious up to a point, that is, not curious enough to be bored for one minute. Writers like Fontenelle, Voltaire and Diderot explained the gravest of concepts in a light, witty conversational style. But soon this charming lightness appeared to evaporate into sheer frivolousness. Nothing could be taken seriously any longer. Montesquieu gave the situation a long look and informed his readers that:

> We banter at Council meetings, we banter leading an army to battle, we banter with an ambassador. . . doctors wouldn't seem ridiculous to us if their clothes looked less gloomy and they bantered as they killed their patients.[1]

This then is the first setting in which we shall seek out the eighteenth-century Frenchwoman—a setting that buried concepts of beauty, passion and profundity under a rococo façade of prettiness. The superficiality of this society that appears in retrospect to have shortchanged itself was to gall Louis Sébastien Mercier in the last years of the century. In his *Tableau de Paris* he exclaimed:

> Fortunate nation with your pretty apartments, your pretty furniture, your pretty jewels, your pretty literary works, eagerly prizing such charming bagatelles. May you prosper forever in your pretty ideas, perfect even more the pretty persiflage that wins you Europe's love, and with your hair forever marvellously dressed, may you never awaken from the pretty dream that gently lulls your lightheaded existence.[2]

Enter the French noblewoman.[3] She enters proudly, for hers is not merely another aristocratic name containing "de." It is an old, illustrious name like Comtesse d'Egmont or Maréchale de Luxembourg. Her friends are called Rohan, Sully, Richelieu, Conti or Boufflers. She has behind her more than the four generations that qualify her as a noblewoman. She can trace her ancestors—but why bother? A genealogist has done it already—at least two centuries back. Perhaps even to feudal times when a grateful king granted some lucky ancestor a duchy or county for services rendered on the battlefield.

Her older brother may be an officer in the army. Other male relatives may hold high ecclesiastical positions. Possibly she has a younger brother, the youngest son whom they call *chevalier.* Perpetually short of cash and with less economic potential than the eldest son and heir, he tries to compensate at the gambling table or at the feet of some bighearted wealthy widow. Not one of her kin works for a living. This would be a scandal in a member of her class. Her family's sources of revenue are usually inheritance money, remuneration for a high office held in government, army or church, royal allowances, or *pensions,* or income from property. All untaxed.

Our lady does not live in the provinces like the obscure impoverished relatives she has never met. Her family might own land in Dordogne or the Vaucluse and journey there occasionally. She might spend weeks or months at Versailles too, dancing attendance on a queen or princess. But Paris is her home.

She has been presented at court. After the court genealogist carefully examined several family documents and allowed that her illustrious ancestry (or, more precisely, her husband's) could be traced at least to the mid-sixteenth century, she made her grand debut before the Queen at Versailles. The pompous ritual introduced by Louis XIV had become honed to a fine art during the eighteenth century. A good illustration of this is Madame de Genlis' play-by-play account of the preparations for her presentation at the court of Louis XV. Since she had to be officially introduced by a woman who had already been presented to the Queen, Madame de Puisieux did the honors. The day before the ceremony she took Madame de Genlis to Versailles where, as custom had it, they visited the ladies-in-waiting of the royal family. They stayed in the beautiful quarters of Madame de Puisieux's daughter, the Maréchale d'Estrées:

Madame de Puisieux and Madame d'Estrées really persecuted me the
next day, the day I was to be presented; they had my coiffure done three
times, and finally agreed on the style that suited me best, the most Gothic
one. They forced me to put on a lot of powder and rouge, two things I
hated; they had me wear the big corset at lunch, "so I would get used
to it," as they said. Those tremendous corsets left your shoulders bare,
cut into your arms and felt horribly uncomfortable. Besides, they had it
pulled incredibly tight to show off my figure.

Mother and daughter then had the bitterest dispute about my scarf and
how to attach it. They were seated and I was standing and totally exhausted during this debate. They put it on me and took it off at least four
times. Finally the Maréchale won out with the backing of her three
chambermaids, and Madame de Puisieux was furious. I was so tired I
could hardly hold up when we had to go to lunch. At lunch they let me
off without having to wear the large hoop under the skirt, though for a
minute they wondered whether I shouldn't get used to that too.

When the Maréchale's husband saw me, he shouted, "She's got too much
powder and too much rouge; she was a hundred times prettier yesterday!"
Madame de Puisieux asked his opinion on the scarf, which he approved
of, and the whole lunch was spent in discussing my costume. I didn't eat
a thing because I was squeezed so tightly I could scarcely breathe. When
we got up from the table, the Maréchale's husband went to his study and
I was left again in the hands of the Maréchale and Madame de Puisieux
who had me finish dressing, that is, put on my hoop and train, and then
rehearse the curtsies that I had learned from a dancing teacher. . . .[4] My
ladies were very satisfied with this rehearsal. But Madame de Puisieux
forbade me to kick my train gently back when I backed up out of the
room, saying, "That's theatrical." I explained that if I didn't push the
long train back, my feet would get tangled up in it and I'd fall. She
repeated in her dry, imperious voice, "That's theatrical." I kept quiet.
Then while these ladies dressed, I quickly rubbed off a little rouge, but,
unfortunately, just as we were leaving Madame de Puisieux noticed it and
said, "Your rouge has come off but I'll put some more on for you," and
she pulled a compact out of her pocket and put much more rouge on my
face than I had before.[5]

Let us explain that to make a costume with a sufficient train—a
detachable one so that the dress could be worn at home after the
presentation—took around thirty yards of material. We can understand Madame de Genlis' wish to do her preventive kick!

The staging of the presentation ceremony was quite a challenge to a newcomer. This is what was expected of her: she executed her first curtsy from inside the door of the ceremonial hall, before the eyes of the whole assembly. Ater a few steps forward, she made her second bow. A third one was in order when she arrived a few feet from the Queen. Then she had to take off the glove of her right hand and bend down far enough to clutch the hem of the Queen's dress in order to kiss it. The Queen would quickly prevent this action, drawing back a few steps (Later Marie-Antoinette was to develop a graceful gesture for this part of the ceremony: she pushed her skirt back adroitly with one elegant stroke of her fan). Generally speaking, only a woman holding the rank of duchess or higher was spared the hem-kissing gesture at presentation time. Instead, she put out her right cheek, and the Queen lightly brushed hers against it.

This much accomplished, the noblewoman lingered a few moments until the Queen had paid her some polite compliment and made a royal curtsy. This was the signal for retreat. But—patience— the departure had to be made backing up and facing the Queen, all the while performing three goodbye curtsies and praying fervently that the train would behave until the final exit.

The night of her presentation, the favored noblewoman went to the Queen's quarters for card playing or gambling. Then all the women present could play at the Queen's round table, sitting on stools called *tabourets* (ordinarily only duchesses or princesses could sit in the Queen's presence)—but only if they arrived before game time and sat down when the Queen took her place at the table. This event was clearly a high point in the life of an eighteenth-century Frenchwoman, and a consecration. The glory and honor underlined in the presentation ceremony perpetually colored her image of herself. But were such glory and honor totally consistent with her personal history? In order to answer this, let us examine a bit more fully how it was to be an aristocratic Frenchwoman of two centuries ago.

Although she could eventually achieve enormous prestige and power, she started her life as a disappointment. A girl baby? But only a boy could preserve the family name and patrimony. As Jules and Edmond Goncourt put it:

The newborn is merely a girl, and in front of this cradle which contains only a woman's future, the father appears indifferent; the mother suffers like a Queen who expected a Dauphin.[6]

The child is immediately shipped off to the country to live with a nurse, and when she is weaned and returns home she is put in the care of a governess and sleeps in her room. This governess is often not much more than a baby sitter, although she usually teaches her charge to read and write, to say her catechism, to curtsy prettily, stand up straight and be *nice*. In many cases the scoldings are minimal, since Nurse counts on keeping in the good graces of her young lady, who may send her off with a generous sum of money when she grows up and marries.

Contact between mother and daughter is limited to only a few minutes a day. The Prince de Ligne describes a girl's daily visit at her mother's *toilette*. It is eleven o'clock. Maman has just got up. She chats with visiting friends while her attractive maids comb and dress her. Says mother to daughter who has just wished her good morning:

Look at yourself! What's the matter with you? You look terrible today. Go put on some rouge; no don't, you'll stay in today instead.

Then, turning toward a visitor who has just arrived:

How I love that child! Come here and kiss me dear—but you're filthy, go brush your teeth. . . . Now don't start asking me all your questions— you're really impossible.

"Madame," says the visitor, "What a loving Mother!" "What can I do?" the lady answers, "I'm mad about that child."[7]

And the little girl goes back to play with her dolls, dressed up like a doll herself: a mature one, though, a miniature replica of her mother, even down to the whalebone corset. Then, after some months of dancing lessons and a little singing at her clavichord, at seven years of age she leaves home for the eighteenth-century equivalent of finishing school—the convent.

We shall not describe her years in this establishment which became so controversial during the last decades of the century.[8] In general, the convent was a handy solution for keeping a daughter away from the temptations of her parents' sophisticated world and, incidentally, out of their hair. It was, moreover, the stylish thing to do. A young girl would not only be raised with other females of her class there, but might perhaps make some important contacts for herself and her family. And if she could pick up a bit of instruction on the way, so much the better.

As the Goncourt brothers have pointed out, the eighteenth-century French convent was not some ascetic prison but a rather worldly place, since it was a refuge for ladies separated from their husbands or women who were badly disfigured by smallpox (at the time, one-fourth of the female population wore some mark of this disease!). Married pre-adolescents of twelve and thirteen awaited nubility in the convent before joining their husbands. Young residents could visit home frequently or they might see visitors through a grill in the parlor. Theatre, concerts and dance penetrated the convent walls along with a constant stream of news and gossip from the glamorous society that these *pensionnaires* were preparing to enter.

At fifteen or sixteen the aristocratic damsel learns that her convent days are over—she is going home. Nine times out of ten this means that she is getting married. She has never met her fiancé and may not even know his name. So here she is, her head and heart full of romantic notions acquired in the convent, excited and frightened, worldly wise through vicarious information gleaned from forbidden novels and hearsay, sensual perhaps but utterly unsophisticated. Take the case of the ingenuous Cécile de Volanges, a character in Laclos' *Liaisons dangereuses.* She has come home from the convent of the Ursulines and immediately writes her news to her convent companion Sophie Carnay:

> . . . It's not five o'clock yet and I'm not supposed to meet Maman till seven. That's a good long time, if only I had something to tell you! But no one has said a thing to me yet; and if I didn't notice all these preparations and all the women coming to measure and fit me, I'd think it was all just one more piece of gossip from old Joséphine.[9] But Maman has told me so often that a young lady should stay in the convent till she marries that Joséphine must be right, because here I am.
>
> A carriage just pulled up at the door and Maman sent word to me to go to her right away. Suppose it's *the* Monsieur? I'm not dressed, my hand is trembling and my heart is really pounding. I just asked the maid if she

knew who was with my mother. She said, "As a matter of fact it's Monsieur C. . ." And she laughed. I think it's him!! I'll come right back and tell you what happens. Anyway, now I know his name. Well I can't keep them waiting. Goodbye till very soon.

You're really going to make fun of your poor Cécile! Was I ever embarrassed! But you would have fallen for it just like me. When I came into Maman's room, I saw a man dressed in black standing near her. I curtsied as well as I could and then I just stood there without budging. You can imagine how I stared at him. He bowed to me and said to my mother, "Madame, the young lady is charming—I appreciate your generosity more than ever." When I heard that I started to shake so hard I couldn't stand up. I reached for an armchair and sat down blushing horribly and really embarrassed. I was no sooner in the chair when this man was on his *knees* before me. Then your poor Cécile lost her head—I jumped up and let out a piercing shriek—you know, like that day it thundered. Maman burst out laughing and said, "Now what's the matter? Sit down and give your foot to Monsieur!" As a matter of fact, dear Sophie, the Monsieur was a shoemaker. I can't tell you how ashamed I was. Fortunately only Maman was there. I think that when I'm married I'll never use that shoemaker.

Well you have to agree we're really sophisticated! Bye bye. It's almost six o'clock and my maid says I have to get dressed. Goodbye my dear Sophie. I love you as much as if I were still in the convent.[10]

Although in this novel poor Cécile's marriage never took place, in actual cases little time elapsed before a young *pensionnaire* became a bride. Marriages were strategic mergers arranged by parents, the wedding of two distinguished names and of two estates—each party usually hoping for the maximum in financial profit. Some daughters had more freedom than others in the selection of a spouse. Madame de Genlis married secretly and Madame de la Tour du Pin was given her choice (actually, both these women settled only for well-bred noblemen). But these were the happy exceptions. A more classic example was the case of Mimi de Bellegarde. A friend of her family, Monsieur de Rinville, had a distant cousin, Monsieur d'Houdetot, who, he said, was sure to be an excellent addition to the Bellegarde family. So the Bellegardes and the Houdetots went to dinner at Rinville's home. As soon as they all met, the "suitor's" mother, the Marquise d'Houdetot, kissed the whole Bellegarde family. Mimi was seated next to young Houdetot. By the time dessert rolled around, somebody broached the subject of marriage. But then Rinville, thinking that affairs were proceeding too slowly, said, "All you have to do is say yes or no and that's that. Our young count is already in love. Your daughter just has to see if she likes him. What do you say, my pet?"

Someone, trying to inject a little reason into the proceedings, suggested that the families might want a little time to mull it over. Rinville was all in favor of this, so he proposed that the young couple go chat together while the two families discussed the business part of the contract. The parents agreed to it and in a flash Rinville had the ball rolling. He blithely announced that the Marquis d'Houdetot would give his eligible son 18,000 francs* a year and a cavalry company that he had already bought for him, and the Marquise d'Houdetot would hand over her diamonds. Then Monsieur de Bellegarde kindly reciprocated by promising a dowry of 300,000 francs and a share of some inheritance money. The contract was signed that night; the wedding took place the following Monday.[11]

What about Mimi? As everyone knew, except perhaps the bride herself, young d'Houdetot had a mistress whom he didn't consider dropping. As for Mimi, the new Madame d'Houdetot and one of the gentlest, most lovable creatures of her time, she remained steadily faithful almost all through her married life—to her lover, the poet Saint-Lambert.

But nobody expected marriage to be romantic bliss. For a young noblewoman, getting married meant being received into society, going to balls, showing off her diamonds at the opera the Friday after her honeymoon, having fine horses and an elegant carriage, being presented at court, having charge of her own household, in short, being *someone.* It is true that many young sentimentalists, fresh out of the convent, fell madly in love with their husbands, but their fate was, more often than not, similar to that of Madame d'Epinay, whose not always dependable *Mémoires* tell the story of life with an unfaithful husband. Weary of his wife's complaints, Monsieur d'Epinay advised her, "You ought to enjoy yourself a little. Get around in society, start friendships, be like all women of your age—it's the only way to make me happy, dear."[12]

---

*Today approximately $18,000. (Though the *livre* or franc was not always one dollar).

So more likely than not, the young wife takes the hint. After a while, she may bear her husband's children but not his presence. They see each other more and more infrequently. Her days are busy, beginning around eleven o'clock, since only a common *bourgeoise* would let the window blinds be opened before that hour. Then, like her mother, she embarks on a long *toilette:* her maids dress her, perfume her and arrange her hair in the presence of her admiring visitors. According to the writer Mercier, what these visitors admire has really been prepared in a first secret *toilette* that attractive men never see, a hasty session in which the hair is brushed and enough cosmetics are applied to make milady presentable. Whether or not this bit of slander has some truth to it, a three-hour *toilette* is an excellent occasion for informal chats or for buying second-hand jewelry and ribbons from women vendors of a lower class. It is also a good time to impress a prospective lover with a faintly revealing negligee, a pretty foot that just happens to knock off its slipper and all manner of coquetry that only the playwright Marivaux could describe.

After her *toilette,* Madame may dispatch a few letters, take a music lesson or go riding in the Bois de Boulogne. Lunch at three o'clock and she is off making her round of visits in the Faubourg Saint-Germain or the Faubourg Saint-Honoré. Then perhaps a stroll is in order: she can walk with friends in the garden of the Palais-Royal or the Tuileries. In the evening she must decide between the Comédie-Francaise, the opera or comic opera, a masked ball or, if they are in season, the fairs of Saint-Germain or Saint-Laurent with their jugglers, mimes, acrobats and their low-comedy theatre. Or, if she prefers to stay home, she can invite friends to stage one of Paris' latest dramatic hits in her own little theatre, and take the juiciest role herself. Some of the evening may be spent in gambling, a favorite sport of the times. Then, around midnight, she and her friends take time out for supper. This is a magic moment in which clever conversation, sly wit and gaiety are appreciated as much as the chef's skill.

It is three a.m., but why say goodbye? She and her contingent can still go out for a last-minute liqueur. Finally, around five o'clock, she is ready for slumber. Her maids undress her and help her to bed, where she remains until eleven a.m., when the whole hectic cycle starts again.

Choosing a Ribbon at the Toilette (Boucher)

We have been discreet. In all of this description there was scarcely a word about love or love affairs. Wasn't there time? Apparently, even the most crowded days or nights left time enough. A third-rate writer, Desmahis, achieved a certain notoriety by outlining an upper-class lady's amorous journey through life. His article on women in Diderot's famous *Encyclopédie* contains a step-by-step satire of her sentimental education. A young innocent whom he calls Cloé is, like most pretty girls, made for love. But, since she is a refined miss, she is prudently sheltered from temptations. Instead she sits dreaming languorously at her keyboard and her mirror. But wait: Cloé marries at last and is introduced into society. Wherever she goes she is surrounded by stylish fops called *petits-maîtres* who pay her court in the most amusing way. In this milieu Cloé harmlessly displays her charms and becomes a practiced coquette. Next step: she falls in love, hopelessly, passionately, eternally, with the only man in the world. She discovers that her lover is unfaithful. Since she is new at this game she hangs on for dear life, sobs, suffers terribly. Time passes. Despair changes to sadness. Cloé is now ready for a little consolation. Soon another love will surface and then another. She enters her woman-of-the-world period, but she manages to wrap every voluptuous experience in a veil of sentiment. Towards the end of this stage she refuses to get involved in prolonged love affairs since, as she says, she doesn't want to suffer. So she may have a fling as the fancy strikes her but she still speaks of such experiences in romantic terms, never in terms of sheer pleasure. Cloé can go on that way for years. She has a distinguished name and a complaisant husband. But, inevitably, the age for loving finally passes her by. Then when the dance is over she may go home with all sorts of family feelings, even conjugal feelings. Soon we find her devoting hours of her day to church affairs and her confessor. She is, after all, a religious woman, a pious woman. And, by the way, Cloé has become quite a prude.

This satire, an oversimplification of course, was actually not too far from the truth. One glance into any of the myriad memoirs of the era and we see essentially the same story. Plays and novels of the day only bear this out with variations on the same scheme.

But how did society react to a woman with an energetic love life? High society couldn't care less. Cloé and her like were accepted, pitied, consoled, admired, courted by all, on one condition: that

nobody broke any rules of etiquette. A member of the "right" society, of *la bonne compagnie,* could do anything and say almost anything so long as she or he conformed to certain unwritten rules which
were part of *le bon ton.* There was a right tone for love, just as there
was one for conversation.

When a new affair had started in earnest, lovers had certain ways
of letting people know, for example, an exaggerated show of respect
on the gentleman's side, reserve and modesty on the part of his new
mistress. If, or when, he left her for another, no one condemned him
provided he did it right, that is, provided he remained friends with
her, showed her great respect and devotion in front of others and
patiently swallowed her reproaches. Even in a tête-à-tête the Code
prevailed. Madame de Genlis tells the tale of the Chevalier de Durfort who stomped furiously through the halls of the Comédie-Française. He was sure that he had seen his mistress and an acquaintance
of his entering a private loge, wearing masks. Fortunately, the door
to the loge was ajar. Durfort peeked at the couple for a minute, then
went away elated. It couldn't have been his mistress, he announced
triumphantly, because the couple did not belong to *la bonne compagnie.* How could he tell that? The unknown man had crossed his foot
over his lady's, instead of gently raising her foot and putting his
underneath it, as any nobleman of Durfort's society would have
done!

Court etiquette seeped into every aspect of life, and even death.
Louis-Sébastien Mercier spoke of a "mourning thermometer" that
not only regulated a lady's actions and dress after the death of an
acquaintance or loved one, but that stipulated the amount of time she
would allow for the consecutive stages of her public behavior ranging
from asocial grief to oblivion and normality.

So style was everything, and nowhere did style seem more regulated than in conversation. Since conversation was perhaps the main
source of entertainment in this society, a lady paid close attention to
the strategics of the game, so that her public would be perpetually
interested and amused. The novelist Crébillon set the rules down in
his *Egarements du coeur et de l'esprit:*

> A person discussing war may be interrupted by some woman who wants
> to talk about love, and she, in the midst of all the ideas that so noble a
> subject inspires in her (and that she is ever so familiar with), must stop

to listen to a suggestive song; but whoever is singing will give up the floor (to everybody's regret) to a bit of moralizing that someone will hasten to interrupt with a scandalous piece of gossip, which, well told or not, will be replaced by some worn-out reflections on music or poetry. . . .[13]

Backbiting was not banished from good conversation. But, again, it was the way you did it that mattered. It seemed politic to spread the slander as equally as possible among a group, so that no one person would appear too villainous. And of course one had to demolish the reputation of those absent as subtly and cleverly as possible. When it came to those present, sharp-tongued females like the Duchesse de Montmorency could disembowel them with one word, but most women of her class tried to utter nothing directly hurtful or embarrassing to their acquaintances. Although they could be vivacious and witty, their aim was to project politeness and discretion. This seemed especially true when they received friends in their own home.

Many writers of the day attempted to describe the way upper-class women spoke, but it is difficult to recapture this style exactly. Some observers reported that they spoke softly and sometimes affected a slight lisp. Jean-Jacques Rousseau, on the other hand, severely criticized some liberated Parisiennes of the highest society who swore like troopers. But for most contemporary witnesses the words "good taste" and "decency" characterized a court noblewoman's speech (at least in public). In chatting with others she kept well within the perimeters of *le bon ton,* and she could become indignant if others stepped over the line. She may have read La Fontaine's licentious short stories and Voltaire's seamy *La Pucelle,* but she would rarely admit it.

In general, the well-trained noblewoman colored her speech with a brand of warmth and graciousness that put others at ease. A word that almost all writers use to describe this tone is "natural." Almost any prominent and admired Frenchwoman of the century is said to have had this natural manner of speaking. Spontaneity and simplicity reigned at the top, but this naturalness was an art too; the aristocratic Frenchwoman was a highly polished "method" actress who imitated artlessness to perfection.

Crébillon summed up this skill when he said that it required "a cultured but unpedantic mind, elegance without affectation, gaiety and freedom without vulgarity and indecency."[14]

So the eighteenth-century French noblewoman lived in a world governed by form and style. The etiquette that modeled her thinking and behavior came to acquire more reality than her motives and actions. Clearly, the overwhelming impact of the Code made for a topsy-turvy scale of values. Society would accept perfidy, infidelity, ingratitude, outrageous lying and cheating, so long as it was all done in good form, that is, cloaked in noble and gracious manners.

These then are some of the highlights and sidelights in the life of an eighteenth-century woman of French court circles. A relative nonenity from birth to marriage, shunted from nurse to governess to convent, timid and generally frightened of her parents and the world —only with marriage does she finally *become* someone. The change is radical. She is not merely her husband's shadow: she can go where she wants, think what she thinks and do pretty much as she pleases.[15] Power and prestige are hers for the taking. She will make visits, write letters and pull every string possible to obtain some royal office or money for a charming male friend or her not-so-charming husband. She can sponsor artists or meddle in politics. Madame de Tencin for one was an expert in political manoeuvers and greatly responsible for the rising star of her brother the Cardinal. The Duc de Choiseul came to power largely through the persistent efforts of his female public relations team: his mother, his wife, his sister and even his mother-in-law. Madame de Tencin's advice to the ambitious writer Marmontel was "Take women, not men, for friends."[16] Here is Montesquieu's assessment of the situation, as set down in his satirical *Lettres persanes:*

> When I arrived in France I found the late King Louis XIV absolutely governed by women, and yet, at his age, I think that of all the monarchs on earth, he was the one who needed it least. One day I heard a woman say "I must do something for that young colonel; I know what he's worth; I'll speak to the minister about him." Another said, "It's surprising that this young abbot has been overlooked. He should be a bishop. He's well born and I can answer for his morals. . ." These women form a kind of republic whose ever active members give each other mutual help and services. It's like a new State within the State.[17]

As we shall see, such exaggeration is set on a solid foundation of truth. But we must leave our blue-blooded gynocracy for the moment to descend a step on the social ladder: let us consider the eighteenth-century *bourgeoise.*

The Bourgeoise

Is it possible to generalize about women of the eighteenth-century French bourgeoisie? The court noblewoman with all her individuality was nevertheless a member of a caste that held a predetermined image of itself, shared much the same rights and privileges and followed the same sacrosanct rituals. On the other hand the eighteenth-century French bourgeoises represented a wide spectrum of milieus and many different levels in the hierachy of social respectability. A somewhat arbitrary but convenient way of imposing order on this sociological chaos is to divide the class into traditional categories of upper, middle and lower (or *haute, moyenne* and *petite)* bourgeoisies.

Enjoying the greatest prestige were those women of the *haute bourgeoisie* who considered themselves noble and bore aristocratic names because their families or husbands had recently (that is, within the previous hundred years or so) been lucky enough to obtain titles of nobility. For the upper bourgeoisie social mobility was conceivable indeed, and an ambitious commoner could dream of driving through noble ranks in a black velvet-lined coach decorated with a patrician coat of arms and answering to the name of Monsieur or Madame de . . .

Such a fantasy would have been nearly undreamable in the distant Middle Ages when staunch bourgeois first became distinguished from feudal serfs.[18] In those days such bourgeois were usually satisfied with the right to work freely as merchants and artisans in the growing cities of France. But by the eighteenth century they had found it possible to buy into the nobility and they quickly imitated the life style of the blue bloods. This display of *hubris* infuriated both the old-guard nobles and unpretentious (or jealous) commoners; it provided Molière with a likely target when he mocked the parvenu in his hilarious spoof, *Le Bourgeois gentilhomme.*

Now, some generations later, the ranks of new nobles or *annoblis* had mushroomed, and more and more bourgeois were itching to join the group and cloak their banal identity in a shimmering new title.

This could be done in several ways: by paying hard cash for letters of nobility, by purchasing a high office that carried with it a hereditary title or by a third type of business transaction—marriage.

For women, marriage was often the answer. It made little sense for a bona fide duchess to marry a commoner, since females could not transmit their nobility: almost always they took on their husband's rank. However, a bourgeoise with an impressive dowry and high-reaching parents had little trouble finding some chevalier or marquis with dwindling funds and a decrepit château, willing to share his title for a litle solvency. As Madame de Sévigné's daughter so winningly remarked within earshot of her middle-class daughter-in-law, "Even the most cultivated land can use a little manure!"[19]

Most marriageable of all were the daughters of plutocrats. Financiers, bankers and fabulously wealthy tax collectors called farmers-general or *fermiers-généraux* were the richest and most powerful members of the *haute bourgeoisie.* The most famous financier of the time, Samuel Bernard, married off his daughters and granddaughters to noblemen and sank a total dowry of 800,000 francs into the bargain. Rarely did the daughters of affluent capitalists have to settle for men of their own class. If they had any competition in making a royal match, it was occasionally from rich middle-class widows reluctant to depart for the other world before their daughters or they themselves made a more earthy ascent into aristocracy. The playwright Dancourt paints a merciless picture of such women in *Les Bourgeoises à la mode, Les Bourgeoises de qualité* and *Le Chevalier à la mode.*

Outside of financial circles, important judicial courts called *parlements* provided one of the best entrées into the aristocracy. As with certain important government and municipal offices, a good number of judiciary posts were up for sale and offered buyers a title to be passed on to future generations. Their heirs would be called law nobility—nobility of *la robe.* So middle-class male aspirants studied law and became august peers and presidents of *parlements* in Bordeaux, Toulouse, Dijon or Paris. At that point, they had gone about as far as they could go. True, they enjoyed a certain glory that they could share with wife and children, but—sad fortune!—in all of these cases of recent ennobling, whether by over-the-counter credentials, purchase of high offices or coveted seats in one of the *parlements,* all the titled descendants of new nobles were considered bourgeois by court nobility until enough centuries had gone by (sometimes three or four) for their sordid origins to seep into a comfortable oblivion.

So if a young bourgeoise didn't mind leaving the altar with some starving courtier, it was easier and far quicker for her to reach royal nirvana than it was for a man with generations of "new" nobility already behind him.

Slyly sneered at by old guard patricians, women of the upper bourgeoisie not only imitated their way of life but often lived in higher style. In Paris, it is true, even an enormously wealthy titled bourgeoise could not match the lady of the court, but in the provinces, especially in big *parlement* cities like Grenoble or Bordeaux, she could outdo fading local countesses without batting an eye. Wherever she lived, she enjoyed sumptuous villas, an expensive cuisine, silk gowns concocted by the Queen's couturière—all this and more—but without the insecurities that plagued court nobles with their decreasing revenues or their need for a high-paid (and perchance dishonest) "intendant" to handle their finances. Hers was new money but steady money, and if it was plebeian to speak of it, it was terribly reassuring to have it around. The proud ladies of the court were up to their teeth in debt, charming or sidestepping creditors at every corner. The bourgeoise and her husband didn't borrow and didn't owe.

The economical habits of the bourgeoise were lampooned by nobles like d'Argenson who portrayed her with her keys to the wine cellar, rationing out food to guests, mentally computing how much it cost and "urging you to eat this or that as though it weren't every day you could come across such a spread."[20] But a refined haute bourgeoise would never act that way. Not a trace of concern: one flick of an eyelash and everyone was served to perfection—even if she had gone over the budget sou by sou the night before.

When the moneyed wives of French capitalists imitated court nobility, many readily adopted the vogue of marital infidelity and estrangement. But in the case of a *parlement* wife, such behavior was the exception. Like commoners socially beneath her, she ate, slept and even talked with her own husband and what's more she wasn't ashamed of it. With this conjugal stability reinforcing her bourgeois sense of financial responsibility, it is understandable that the *parlement* wife led a more sober and regulated life than other members of high society. Religion played a strong part here. Members of the law courts and their families were mainly Jansenists who approved of a strict religious code and who (largely for political reasons it is true) bitterly opposed the relatively lax Jesuits reigning at the royal court. Their wives were often devout churchgoers who gave their spare moments to charitable activities and to their confessors or visiting clerics called "conscience directors." Compared with the flashier financiers' wives, however, they were more apt to play a strong role in public affairs. They could be passionately interested in politics and were not always content to watch events from the sidelines. Léon Abensour has seen in this group a force "that contributed. . .to the defeat of royal power"[21] and a prerevolutionary force. They demonstrated as a group; they rioted against such opposition figures as the Duc de Fitz-James and the Maréchal de Richelieu; they made themselves heard whenever the existence or well being of their *parlements* was threatened by royalty. These staunch Jansenist bourgeoises were among the most important feminine activists in eighteenth-century France.

While the women of the upper middle class were pole vaulting into noble ranks and beating the old nobility at its own game, another layer of feminine bourgeoisie, the *moyenne,* had other preoccupations and another style of life. For one thing, these middle bourgeoises started out with a completely different upbringing than their patrician counterparts. Most little girls were raised by their own mothers, who dressed them, took them visiting and familiarized them with the running of a household. At around eleven years of age a daughter very likely went off to a convent for the bit of formal schooling and religious instruction that preceded her confirmation. But this was for only a year or two. Soon she was back home leading what the Goncourt's have called her "double life."[22] On the one hand she received private lessons in music, dance, geography or penmanship—thus learning the same subjects as "finer" young ladies; on the other she went marketing with a servant or her mother and helped around the kitchen—thus performing the same chores as a common cook (the "Cinderella" aspect, however, was more characteristic of the *petite* than of the *moyenne* bourgeoise).

There is a curious reversal of freedom that becomes apparent when we compare the life of a *moyenne* bourgeoise with that of a noble-woman or *haute* bourgeoise. The middle bourgeoise enjoyed more liberty than those more elegant females who were kept under wraps in a convent until marriage time. She might have met her fiancé at church, at a ball or walking with her family in the Luxembourg Gardens or the Bois de Boulogne. Perhaps he became known to her and her family through relatives or mutual friends. He would ask permission to visit her, and if there was no objection, there he sat, week after week, playing cards and chatting with the nubile miss. The parents stationed themselves within hearing range, and in most cases the fiancée deserved her white wedding dress when the day came—but a little kissing was no crime. Rather than the prompt settling of a deal, marriage here was more likely considered as the wedding of two individuals. The young girl of this class had a greater say in the choice of her mate. She didn't have to be madly in love with him, but chances are that her parents looked for some positive inclination on her part.

But then this pre-marriage freedom was followed by a stricter pattern once the knot was tied. No nonsense here about living apart from your spouse; the moyenne bourgeoise lived with and for her husband. He was possibly a functionary such as town clerk, a professional man like a doctor or lawyer or a business man at the start of a prosperous career. His new wife was proud to be his helpmeet and happy when he discussed his job with her. Perhaps she even took an active part in his work. Restif de la Bretonne claims that by the end of the eighteenth century Parisian bourgeoises had become less involved in their husbands' occupations. But one of his own heroines was a shining example of the bourgeoise wife-associate. This is how his Suzanne spent her free time one day after assigning the household chores in the morning:

> She took advantage of this time to go into the shop. She went up to each of the machinists one after another and inquired kindly about the health of the wives, children, fathers and mothers of these good people. As a child she had observed that when her mother visited the factory work-shop she often wore a tasteless or even dirty housedress and was terribly sloppy. She had heard people make fun of her for that. So when she went to her husband's shop she always showed up in an attractive housefrock.

A Bourgeoise Reading (Liotard)

She had observed that people always worked willingly and accepted most of a woman's criticism if she dressed well. . .

After her rounds Suzanne went back to her servants and set to work with her maids. Then she thought about lunch. Company was often invited, so the preparations gave her a good deal of work. She went at this economically but also like a hostess who wanted to do justice to her husband and to satisfy her guests. She spent only a half hour at her *toilette* because her hair had been done in the morning, because frequent bathing kept her clean and because at lunch time she only had to throw on a dress and change from slippers to shoes. . .

After lunch, while they were still at the table, you could see her gracefully gather together the little glasses, and without getting up, continuing the conversation, rinse them and give them to a servant to dry. Then she went into the kitchen to see that everything was put in order and nothing lost. She came back right away. The gaming tables were set up but just for the guests. She didn't play: she busied herself with sewing instead. When everybody had left she read or had someone read to her while she did some light work. She visited the workers at a different time each day so that they might expect her to show up at any moment.[23]

Our little paragon, it appears, is also a faithful wife, for it is true that fidelity was more customary at her level than at a higher one. If Suzannes like this were tempted, at least they usually tried not to follow through. And unlike a *haute* bourgeoise or a noblewoman, a *moyenne* could be seen taking her husband's arm and overheard calling him "lamb" or "sweetie."

Was she her husband's equal? Although we cannot measure categorically the conjugal balance of power in the *moyenne bourgeoisie,* we know that in Paris the average middle-class woman was more frequently on a par with her mate than in the provinces, where she most often played the part of respected subordinate. Her participation in his work could sometimes amount to a true partnership; for example, her husband might need her countersignature on contracts. But morally she was rarely considered his equal.

Occasionally the *moyenne* bourgeoise distinguished herself in a more brilliant role than that of roost ruler or helpmeet: witness Madame Geoffrin, who came to wield great influence as director of her famous Paris salon. But most women of her social background could not dream of competing with upper-class ladies in political or

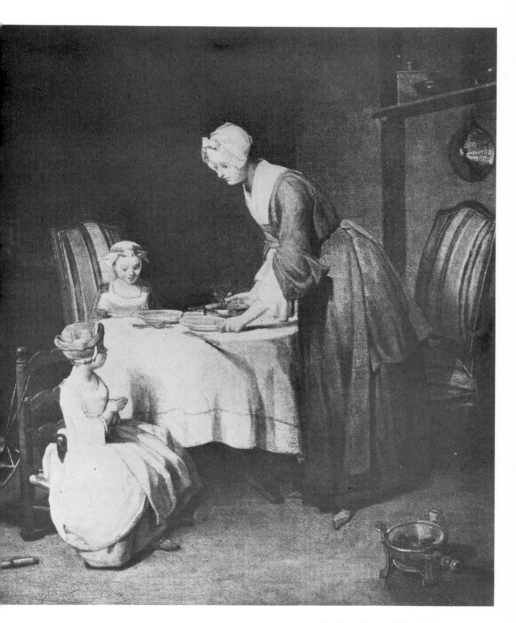

Saying Grace (Chardin)

artistic authority and prestige. For them the more customary conduits to success were in economy and industry. Some women, married or not, owned productive pieces of land which they themselves administered. Others held important jobs such as postmistress or hospital director or filled certain municipal posts and bureaucratic positions in the field of finance. Some even tried to infiltrate into medicine which, like law, was legally closed to women. A good number of widows enjoyed flourishing careers, often carrying on where their late husbands had left off: running factories, selling grain, opening and exploiting mines, starting new businesses or holding local offices. They were especially active in the manufacture, sale and exportation of silk and other fabrics.

As the century and the standard of living progressed, many an average bourgeoise could live as fast and as high as the social elite. Then we might even find our good Suzanne rejecting conjugal duties (as well as shop inspection) as clearly unworthy of the fine lady she saw smiling disdainfully from her bedroom mirror. Yet even in the waning century, writers like Diderot, La Chaussée and Mercier could still hold the bourgeoise up to her "superiors" as an edifying example of conscientious mother and spouse.

A more colorful segment of the middle class was the *petite bourgeoisie*. Women of this group were wives and daughters of tradesmen, shopkeepers, artists or small property owners in the provinces, most of whom made a fair but not impressive living. Their upbringing followed much the same pattern as that of the *moyenne bourgeoisie* but with greater emphasis on household tasks. It is the *petite* bourgeoise who graces the realistic paintings of Chardin, a modest daughter near the unadorned skirts of her attentive mother, surrounded not by drapes or statues but by equipment for cooking and tidying their simple and clean interior.

In the seventeenth century the kitchen had been their "salon." In that room the petite bourgeoise had cooked and served meals and chatted with her visitors. Now, however, on those occasions when she had company, they sat in a separate room, an unpretentious, neat livingroom, decorated perhaps with mirrors and a few paintings. There she could gossip with intimates about her domestic problems and, especially, those of her neighbors. Her viewpoint was conservative; if she had a philosophy, it was synonymous with tradition and it focused on such familiar concepts as religion, family and work.

Marivaux has captured the chatty, next-door-neighbor petite bourgeoise at home in his portrait of Madame Alain of his novel *Le Paysan parvenu.* This worthy woman has rented out rooms to a mature spinster and her young peasant protégé. When they confide to her that they are planning to get married secretly, her response is a surprised "To each other?" But she is simply burning to help them and promises to be the soul of discretion.

"And why would anybody talk anyway? Because of your age? Well, good grief, what's wrong with that? Last week wasn't there a woman of at least seventy in our parish who got engaged to a twenty-year-older? Age should only concern the people involved. That's their business."

"I'm not so very old," said Mademoiselle Habert, still embarrassed.

"Good grief no," said her hostess. "You're still of marriageable age, that is, now or never. After all, to each his own. If your intended happens to be young, so take him young. . . he'll have enough youth for both of you. Ten years more, ten years less. . . What can people say anyhow? That you could be his mother? Well, the worst of that is that he could be your son. If you had one maybe he wouldn't be so good looking and he'd be a lot more trouble. Don't worry about people gossiping and tell me all about your affair."[24]

The air of easy familiarity that was natural in a petite bourgeoise like the garrulous Madame Alain could drop in a split second when a woman of her class was pitted against someone she considered her inferior. At the bottom rung of the bourgeoisie, a woman could still consider herself higher than the proletariat and would insist on doing so. Again, let us turn to the incomparable Marivaux for a near tape recording of a petite bourgeoise's tone and manner. Madame Dutour, a shopkeeper in *La Vie de Marianne,* sees her charge, the orphan Marianne, roll up to her linen goods store in a public carriage like a real lady. Marianne starts to pay the cabbie, But Madame Dutour, eager to show what a woman of experience she is, insists:

"Let me do it. I'll pay him. Where did he pick you up?"

"Near the church. . ."

"Oh, that's right near here," she answered, counting out some change. "Here, sonnie, this is for you."

"This is for me! That!" said the driver, who gave her back her change with brutal disdain. "Uh-uh, no sir. You don't go measuring rides by the yardstick."

"Now what is this man talking about with his 'yardstick'?" Madame Dutour replied solemnly. "You should be satisfied with that. I think I know what a cab ride is. Today isn't the first time I've paid for one, you know."

"So even if it was tomorrow, what difference does that make? Gimme my money and don't yak so much. Look at her sticking her nose in it. Did I drive you? Did anybody ask you anything? What the hell kind of woman is she with her twelve cents! She acts like a street vendor haggling over a bunch of herbs."

Madame Dutour was proud, all dressed up and pretty good looking to boot, all of which imbued her with a sort of glory. . . The "bunch of herbs" offended her ears. How could words like that come to the lips of anyone who saw her? Was there anything in her looks that could make you think a thing like that?

"Really, my friend, I must say you are very impertinent, and I'm not about to stand here and listen to your stupid talk. All right, go on now. Here's your money, take it or leave it. What is this? If I call my neighbor that'll teach you to speak to the bourgeois more decently."

"Now now, what's this ragpicker's wife telling me?" answered the fellow, as only a cabbie can. "Look out, there, get a load of her. She has her Sunday shawl on. Wouldn't you think you have to bow down to talk to Madame?. . . Now damn it, pay me. If you was four times more bourgeoise, what do I care? Don't my horses have to live? What would you eat on, you, if you didn't get paid for your cloth? Aah, it's disgusting to be such a cheapskate!"[25]

A bad example can lead you astray. Madame Dutour, who had remained within the bounds of middle-class dignity until then, could not resist after that last insult from the driver. She dropped the fruitless respectable lady role, let her hair down and resorted to the style of quarreling that she was used to, that is, to the language of an ordinary shop counter biddy. She didn't spare the horses.

But we shall spare the reader the sight of Madame Dutour un-
leashed and armed with her fabric store yardstick. Actually, in more
cases than not the trend was reversed, and rather than descending
from mediocre heights to the level of the rabble, the petite bourgeoise
bettered herself during the eighteenth century. As she became increasingly affluent she attempted to follow the example of high
society. Merchants' wives could afford luxurious furniture and even
precious jewels, and their traditional serge gave way to silks and
velvets. By the end of the century, as Restif de la Bretonne said
admiringly, the Parisian petite bourgeoise was setting the style for
France and all of Europe.

Like the middle bourgeoise, she scarcely played any political role
in her times, but was highly energetic on the domestic front and in
business and industry. Most merchants' wives truly collaborated
with their mates and worked alongside them at their jobs. They sold
at counters, kept the books, took charge of the correspondence and
had a detailed knowledge of the business. Certain of them, especially
widows like Madame Dutour, kept their own shop or directed small
businesses or factories where they busied themselves ordinarily in the
production and sale of lace, silk and other fabrics. Some, like
Madame Alain, ran rooming houses. But not all could make ends
meet, and a good number of these women struggled along rather
painfully or even retired to convents.

Still, depressing as life in this class could be, a petite bourgeoise
was, after all, a petite bourgeoise, and that was some consolation. She
was still "respectable," a member of the worthy middle class and a
good step up from riffraff whom she could refer deprecatingly to as
la canaille.

The Lower-Class Woman

Le peuple was a more polite term to use for the lower classes who
comprised the vast majority of the French population. Censuses were
rare and undependable at the time, but a population study of 1709
revealed that out of approximately 19,094,144 inhabitants of France,
300,000 were nobles, 1,800,000 bourgeois and 16,944,144 lowly
members of the proletariat.[25] Although theoretically all non-nobles
were part of this plebeian estate, the bourgeois had climbed so far

The Market at Place Maubert

that now the word *peuple* meant largely those hardworking, hard-drinking plebs who labored with their hands, hawked and begged in the streets or did menial tasks.

In Paris the narrow, dirty streets swarmed with these men and women. They joked, squabbled and ran errands over slippery cobblestones and through mud puddles, deftly evading coaches and those fast carriages known as *cabriolets* that flashed lethally between, around and occasionally over them. They filled the air with noise. Taverns resounded with their chatter and haranguing; the streets rang from morn to night with the muddled cries of vendors and charlatans.

Here we discover another breed of woman. The grace and femininity exuded by the upper and middle classes were rare commodities in this milieu. Lower-class females were toughened by hard work, the sun and the wind. You could see them, muscular and masculine, haggling in the market of Les Halles, strong-arming some unprepossessing bourgeois to buy at their stalls. Their language was picturesque to say the least (even virgins knew—and used—obscenities that would curdle your blood). Like their men they were curious about everything and everyone. Marivaux caught them running to the scene of Madame Dutour's quarrel with the cabbie, gaping, discussing, interfering, taking sides, and he concluded, "The people of Paris are more *peuple* than other people."[26]

A whole cross-section of Parisian women of the lower classes parades through the short stories of Restif de la Bretonne. In *Les Contemporaines* Restif names well over 200 of their numerous occupations. He refers to almost all of them as "pretty" or "little": "the pretty fruit vendor," "the pretty seamstress," "the pretty milkmaid," "the little needle vendor," "the little cosmetics seller." And yet, with all his idealization, he understands their foibles too, their somber resentments, their quick vengeance followed by their equally quick remorse, their refuge in alcohol.

Less precise in recording the syntax and pronunciation of a lower-class woman, Métra, the author of a *Correspondance secrète,* was perhaps more adept than Restif in conveying her style and thought. Here is his portrayal of such a woman as she explains the circumstances of her recent widowhood. Someone asks her how her husband is and she replies:

Very good sir, oh very good. Poor dear man, they buried him yesterday.
Thursday morning he says to me, "I'm choking!" "You're choking, poor
Jackie (I used to call him that sometimes for fun). Didn't I tell you, it's
your asthma. Well go on, *breathe,*" I says. "I can't" he says. "Yes you
can, don't be such a sissy." Good Lord am I sorry I came out with that,
'cause he couldn't, it bowled him over like lead. I made him take a swig
of that hyacinth confession juice. . .it cost 32 cents, no more no less. Not
that I hold it against him, poor dear man. But he couldn't get it down.
When I see that I says to him, "Hey Jack, suppose I get the priest?" "If
you want to," he says. So I send for the priest and he confesses, poor dear
man. He was as innocent as a baby, same as a baby. Then after he
confesses I says to him, "You see Jack, it's like insurance—you don't
know who's gonna live or die, you see. It doesn't help or hurt you." Then
they take sweet Jesus to him at 10:00 o'clock and he's pretty quiet. . . A
minute later he yells "Woman, woman!" "Well what do you want?" I
says, "Good God, the pans are turning around." he says. I had some pans
on the wall in front of his bed. Lordy me! So I run out and call the
neighbors. When I get back he's already dead. Who would've guessed it,
poor man. . . and now I have to give everything back to the Company,
even his ties. I lost two of them or maybe he sold them for a swig of
brandy. That was his only fault, poor man. No more man, good Lord,
no more man! He never talked to me but it was a consolation to have him
around.[27]

These lower-class women were, in some ways, much freer than the
bourgeoises. In Paris many were sent out at eighteen years of age or
earlier to work in shops, sell merchandise in the streets or become
domestics. When writers describe a young miss on her own in Paris
nine times out of ten they are thinking of the most refined member
of the working class, the fashion shop worker, traditionally dressed
in grey serge and called therefore *grisette*. Mercier speaks wistfully
of the frail and pretty coquette, sewing hats or dresses as she sits at
her shop window in full view of passersby, slyly watching herself be
watched.

Housed away from her family, the guess is that a teenage *grisette*
found a male friend, some young student perhaps, or a not-so-young
but rich Monsieur. If she was good looking and ambitious, some
grateful gentleman might repay a year or two of her favors with a
dowry that enabled her to marry above her station. But this was not
always the case, and when it came to proletarian girls working in less

acceptable surroundings than the *grisette*'s, social climbing to any real heights was rare,[28] and illegitimate offspring were frequent.

If married, the lower-class woman was, even more than the bourgeoise, her husband's helper. Whether by his side or elsewhere, she would toil long hours to supplement his meager income. Her work gave her, on the one hand, a certain freedom of movement and at times a degree of financial independence, but more often than not it made a sheer slave of her. And a woman's drudging, no matter how much it earned, brought in less pay than a man's. The rule was that a female could rarely live on what she alone earned: the male income would help her get through.

Outside the bustling realm of Paris lived the great majority of the lower classes. Unlike the Parisian *peuple* they earned their livelihood less from the production and sale of commodities than from cultivating the precious land around them. Instead of following English capitalists and workers toward an industrial revolution, the French, encouraged by eighteenth-century physiocrats like Quesnay, put their faith and emotional investment into their rich soil. Beyond Parisian boundaries, consequently, the workers remained largely peasants and farmers.

Since agricultural tasks could be strenuous, a peasant woman's work was mainly confined to household tasks or to relatively nonmuscular activities in the fields and around truck farms, chicken coops or cowstalls. Occasionally she had a job outside of agriculture: selling fabrics, meat or salt, tending a cabaret or working as a washerwoman, midwife, wetnurse, servant and even a paid mourner at funerals.

Within this large class of peasant families the standard of living varied tremendously. Many suffered acutely from intense poverty and hunger aggravated by a whole series of famines that plagued France in the 1700's.[29] Some luckier ones could manage quite comfortably in well-furnished homes stocked with a goodly supply of food, linens and country clothes. Wives of industrious farmers like Restif's father gave supper regularly to around twenty-two people including their ploughmen, vineyard workers and shepherds, their servants and their children.

Until the final decade and its Revolution, a small number of females were still actually serfs who, like their husbands, could be

Milkmaid (Greuze)

bought and sold with the property they worked on. Yet this was a rare phenomenon. Women and men were free, although both were obliged to pay all manner of extraordinarily heavy taxes and duties. On the farm wives were usually legal partners; a farmer's spouse was his co-farmer who entered into all of his business transactions. After all, she ordinarily brought to the marriage a dowry consisting of a little house and field and perhaps some healthy livestock to boot. And yet. . .

And yet how many peasant women had legitimate grounds for complaint! Those who worked for a living not only earned far below Paris standards; they also had to contend with great discrepancies between male and female salaries. In Berry, for example, women employed in making hay received three sous a day and in Guyenne five sous, while men earned twelve for the same work. Even in cases where a woman worked side by side with her husband as his associate or partner, she was still considered his subordinate. When the average farmer's wife served dinner, she would often serve the farmer first, then all his hired help, and finally, she herself ate—standing up—the remains of the meal. Small wonder that a priest of Auvergne declared that the French peasant "took care of his cow more readily than his wife."[30]

It was when a wife became a widow that her stock could go up. She might lament "No more man!" as did her Paris cousin bereaved of "poor Jackie," but then she usually took over the farm or job that he had dominated and managed what money came in. What a temptation to be a widow!

Whether in the provinces or in Paris, servants were considered near the rock bottom of the lowest class, for beneath them crouched only beggars, street prostitutes and criminals. Yet even within the servant class a social hierarchy was apparent. Among the most respected of female domestics was the woman in charge of a large household of servants, or the *gouvernante,* whose word could be near to law for those servants under her wing. The wet nurse too was a favored employee. She was usually a non-Parisian, since it seemed healthier to keep new babies out in the unpolluted countryside. Hired nursing mothers were generally treated well in the hope that babies would thrive in their care. Another relatively well-off member of the household staff was the lady's maid in Paris high society (the *sui-*

vante or *soubrette* of French comic theatre) who could often parade
about in Madame's castoff silks and satins and could adopt the
refined tone of her employers.

But there were maids and maids. In Paris, ladies' maids could be
highly specialized, one girl acting as *coiffeuse,* another as make-up
expert and still another in charge of dressing Madame at her *toilette.*
In the provincial *moyenne* or *petite bourgeoisie,* however, a female
servant was often *the* servant, in charge of everything and very like
a member of the family.

Cooks could command a good price. Early in the century most
cooks were males, but toward the end females came to occupy more
and more culinary positions in the homes of wealthy French families.
With France's great emphasis on "l'art de la cuisine," it is not
surprising that these women were fairly well paid.

Then there was the abundant female army of hired hands: cleaning
women, scullery maids or the waitresses at dingy inns, each one of
whom served hundreds of dishes to over a hundred customers in a
typical day. And if such women could be poorly paid in Paris, they
received next to nothing in the hinterlands of the nation.

Most Parisian women domestics were recruited from the provinces as young girls. Some of them had come to the big city hoping
to find a niche in the flourishing fashion industry and, failing, had
wound up as menials. Their overall image had changed radically
since the seventeenth century when people spoke more readily of the
old, faithful family servant. Now the women hirelings like the men
had a reputation for untrustworthiness, and the turnover in servants
of both sexes was unusually rapid. Fluctuations in France's economy
in the early decades of the century encouraged this trend. When John
Law's system of paper money touched off a hectic speculation during
the Regency, some Parisian valets made a fortune in one day. French
menials could now dream of bettering themselves and leaving the
serving class for good. The plays of Regnard and Lesage offer striking examples of this social upheaval: servants who are fired or leave
in a huff, only to triumph on another stage. As the valet Frontin said
of his bourgeois master Turcaret in Lesage's play of that name:
"Monsieur Turcaret's reign is over; mine has just begun." Every
Frontin had his Lisette who was as ready as he to find happier
hunting grounds in the bourgeoisie.

Kitchen Maid with Lice (Lancret)

Two groups of ladies there were whose bank accounts could on occasion make a *haute bourgeoise* faint with envy. Although these women could also be quite poor, historians include them in the lower-class category not for economic but for moral reasons. Their life's work revolved around the esthetic or the sexual, for they either took to the stage or they made their living horizontally. And we might add that some enterprising females combined both professions successfully. Whether virtuous or not, actresses were not considered much more respectable than prostitutes. This may seem strange to us today when, thanks to Stanislavsky, Copeau and others, acting has been elevated to a serious art form. But at the time, French playgoers viewed the profession with other eyes. Women had only performed regularly in public since the seventeenth century. What is more, the Church had condemned theatre as deleterious to public morals, and actors were literally excommunicates, deprived of the right to Christian sacraments. To Voltaire's dismay, even the famous tragedienne Adrienne Lecouvreur could not officially be buried in holy ground. Working in close quarters with men and emoting with them in romantic fictions, these women, seeing themselves ostracized by the Church, were all the more encouraged to live outside the law.[31]

This did not mean that actors and actresses were universally despised. On the contrary, they were in spite of—and sometimes because of—their reputation, the idols of the day. The mania for theatre was rampant in eighteenth-century France. Diderot and other authors of the day wrote tracts on the actor's juggling of art and reality. Voltaire invited the famous Mademoiselle Clairon to perform his works in the little theatre of his Swiss mansion. Actresses, like actors, rushed off to Versailles at the King's command. They were sometimes called his slaves, since they could be thrown in prison if they disobeyed his orders (Clairon did actually go to jail when she refused to appear in a certain play at the Comédie-Française). Still they were wined, fêted and even worshipped by royalty and commoners alike.

Women in this field took on more and more professional responsibility. A century before, a woman had already directed the most famous troupe in France—she was Armande Béjart, Molière's widow. Now, women directors were very much in evidence; they organized tours in the provinces and productions in the capital. Moreover, since the organization of the Comédie-Française in 1680, the board of actors that chose scripts and directed plays was one-half women. These actresses, outspoken and influential, perpetually upstaged the author, not only passing judgment on his play but reshaping it to suit their own talents.

When that incomparable entrepreneuse Madame de Pompadour constructed a royal theatre as a showcase for her own charm and virtuosity, the statutes of her noble troupe were a blatant example of sexual discrimination—against men. Here are a few of her regulations:

Only actresses will have the right to choose a work that the troupe will stage.

They will also have the right to set the dates of performances and the number, time and day of rehearsals.

Each actor will be obliged to be exactly on time at rehearsals under penalty of a fine that the actresses will decide together.

Only actresses will have a half-hour's grace, after which time their fine will be decided by them alone.[32]

Such official favoritism was, of course, unusual and not to be expected outside the caprice of a King's mistress. But on the whole actresses in France were considered every bit the equal of actors.

Taken much less seriously than the dramatic actress was the female performer at the Opéra. The term "filles de l'Opéra" could always provoke a knowing smile. These were the women of scandalous repute, most of them less talented than the celebrated opera dancer, La Camargo, or the singer, Mademoiselle Fel, but every bit as affectionate as they. When Rousseau told in his *Confessions* how his ex-friend Grimm became sick for love of Miss Fel, he added, "It would really have been a marvellous ancedote if the cruelty [read "chastity"] of a *fille de l'Opéra* led a man to die of despair."[33] One of the sharpest satires on the subject is found in Montesquieu's *Lettres persanes.* It is a translucent proposition from the pen of an aging opera dancer without enough charms left to supplement her artistic income in the boudoirs of Paris.

Dear Sir:

I am the unhappiest girl in the world. I have always been the most virtuous actress in the Opéra. Seven or eight months ago I was in the private loge where you saw me last night. Since I was dressed as the priestess Diana, a young abbot came to see me there, and without respect for my white dress, my veil and my diadem, he ravished my innocence. It was no use stressing the sacrifice that I made. He burst out laughing and assured me that he found me very profane. However, I am so big now that I don't dare appear on stage, for I am highly sensitive on the subject of honor, and I always maintain that a respectable girl would prefer to lose her virtue than her modesty. What with this delicacy on my part, you can understand that this young abbot would never have succeeded had he not promised to marry me, and such a legitimate motive made me bypass the ordinary little formalities and begin where I should have ended. But since his faithlessness has dishonored me, I am through with life at the Opéra, where, between you and me, I hardly get enough to live on, because now that I am getting older and somewhat less attractive, my salary, which is just the same as before, seems to get smaller every day.

I have learned from someone in your entourage that dancers are highly prized in your country and that, if I were in Ispahan my fortune would be guaranteed. If you would grant me protection and take me with you to that country, you would be helping out a girl whose virtue and behavior would prove worthy of your kindness. Very truly yours.[34]

It was at the Opéra especially that the aristocrats of Paris courtesans were formed and sought out, and that an esthetic profession combined with a sexual one. If this was harlotry, it was harlotry at a high level, for these beauties were courted and kept by wealthy noblemen, farmers-general and foreign admirers. At times the competition for the musical hetaeras smacked of an auction. In 1768, for example, the Prince de Condé and the Comte de Lauraguais competed for the opera dancer Mademoiselle Hingre. The Comte won out with an offer of 60,000 francs. Milady's upkeep could be exorbitant what with her craving for well-appointed town houses and carriages and the wardrobe, jewels and allowance necessary to keep her interested. Yet, for so many upper-class men, this luxury was a downright necessity. Actresses of the Comédie-Francaise were also attractive prey, but far less elegantly kept than the "filles de l'Opéra."

At what point did love become prostitution? Certainly, outside the glamorous universe of theatre and opera, women were kept by men. Voltaire spent thousands on Madame du Châtelet and on his ample, voluptuous niece Madame Denis, and neither woman confined her amorous activities to Voltaire. But prostitution then as now was not simply getting rewarded for sex; it meant engaging regularly in the profession (as a profession) of selling oneself to any and all customers (as customers). Although in principle courtesans and kept women were engaging in the same sport, they considered themselves miles apart from the scores of professionals who solicited on city streets. These streetwalkers were largely girls of the *peuple* who had been recruited or seduced into their career. A good number of them had come to Paris from the provinces with a few francs in their pockets and perhaps the address of some distant relative, hoping in vain to make a decent living. Some were orphans or local girls abandoned by their parents. And many preferred prostitution to available menial jobs with their salaries of only twelve sous a day.

Mercier estimated that there were 20,000 to 30,000 prostitutes in Paris, earning fifty million francs a year among them. But most of this money went to dressmakers, jewelers and various other creditors, and often to the police for payoffs. Pimps, too, demanded their due. Although they did not necessarily do any soliciting, these men, called *souteneurs,* made a living by "protecting" the ladies of the night. But rather than discuss the sordid *souteneur,* the eighteenth-century French writers prefer to describe the *greluchon:* a lover who lived on his girl friend's earnings. It was, in fact, this system that the fickle Manon Lescaut proposed to her beloved Des Grieux.[35]

The Profession may have done wonders for the nation's economy, but its abuses were many and far-reaching. End-of-the-century writers such as Restif de la Bretonne and Louis Sébastien Mercier pleaded for reform. Restif, especially, protested against the seduction of innocent girls and the wholesale spread of venereal disease, and in his *Pornographe* he set forth a detailed proposal for a government sponsored program of legalized prostitution (such a daring suggestion was not to be taken seriously until the twentieth century).

The Palais-Royal gardens were the regular stomping grounds of demi-monde adventuresses, who promenaded regularly there at 5:00 p.m. If the well-born ladies of Paris were dismayed to see these creatures walking past them or lolling brazenly on nearby benches, at least they were spared the sight of the common street walker. Since most women of that class did not have a decent wardrobe, they wouldn't dare compete with the courtesan on display. They did their business around Porte Saint-Denis, Porte Saint-Martin and in front of certain cabarets, or they sat at windows and balconies hissing their familiar "st, st, st" at prospective customers. Many took lodgings in furnished rooms near the Palais-Royal, where they had to pay twice the price ordinarily charged for the room, and they paid in advance. When a girl had only one dress, one clean slip and one pair of shoes, she could hardly go out soliciting over treacherous cobblestones and risk total inundation in the mudholes of Paris. So she employed an old bawd called a *marcheuse* to drum up trade. Another lass might use the call-girl system, leaving her address on file with a procuress who delivered her by coach directly to the doorstep of some sedentary gentlemen. And there were seraglios too where girls were nicknamed like horses in a stable, for their personality or physical makeup: Artificial, Proud, Mincing, Darling, Chubby and even Limpy. To add a little spice for jaded clients, a city seamstress or laundress might pose as a naïve peasant girl fresh from the village.

An unwritten but respected law held that no virgin could be taken into a bordello. As Mercier said, "she had to be deflowered first."[36] Those who did make the grade were housed and kept in line by the madam whom they called "mother" and who was rarely arrested. Instead the police made regular raids on whatever prostitutes they could track down. An ordinary *fille* was perpetually menaced by the law. She could be hauled off the streets, taken half dressed from her room and transported to jail in an open wagon. She had no lawyer, no spokesman; only a judge sealed her fate. If he so decreed, her future might be the feared hospital-prison La Salpêtrière. Or if she failed a medical examination, she was shipped off to the horrible Hôpital La Bicêtre. Then in prison, they shaved off her hair, dressed her in sackcloth and wooden shoes, housed her most often in an unheated room, fed her only bread and soup and forced her to work beyond the point of exhaustion. At Bicêtre, prostitutes with venereal disease were herded like livestock into incredibly close quarters along with all sorts of sick inmates. Needless to say, more than a few ended their lives there. For others the destination might be America. During the first two decades of the century, especially, the French government had endorsed the deportation of prostitutes from institutions such as La Salpêtrière to colonies like Mississippi or—as in the case of the fictional Manon Lescaut—Louisiana.

Police Arresting Prostitutes for Deportation

For a girl who wanted to stay in business and yet avoid the specter of the *hôpital,* her best insurance was indeed the stage. If she was pretty enough and ambitious enough, she might be discovered and find sanctuary at the Opéra or the Comédie-Française, where until 1774 any female artist was legally "in absolute possession of her person," and consequently safe from police raids.[37] Small wonder that so many prostitutes were stage struck, and even less wonder that a goodly number of them realized their dream. After all, the theatre director was generally a man. Besides, in the opera dance corps, at least, talent was not a prerequisite. Three months of lessons would enable the initiate to muddle it through as a daffodil in the back line of a ballet. The abundance of these gauzy, ethereal, semi-nude ex-hookers on the stage of the Opéra only served to confirm its reputation as a high-class brothel.

If the lowly harlot could ascend to stardom and security, the reverse was, unfortunately, just as true. A bejeweled hetaera in vogue at one moment could suddenly find herself out of favor, bereft of everything and back on the streets counting her sous. Within this class of wanton women, social mobility was most possible, most rapid and most turbulent.

What significance did the lower-class woman have in the context of eighteenth-century France? It is certain that working women, both in Paris and the provinces, played a vital part in the economic and professional life of the country. Wherever industry was developing, whether in Paris, Amiens, Lyons or Caen, womanpower was in demand. Impecunious old maids, peasants or widows not only supplemented men's work but contributed their own special skills and flair in lacemaking, sewing, designing, making and selling feminine adornments such as artificial flowers and fans.

Since the Middle Ages, French industry was organized around artisans' guilds called "corporations." Some of these were traditionally all-female, for example, the corporations of silk weavers, wool weavers, embroiderers, seamstresses, fabric sellers and wax candle vendors. Sometimes male corporations gave them trouble. The male *fripiers* (sellers of used clothing) stormed against the corporation of female vendors at *toilettes.* Fabric salesmen harrassed women embroiderers who decorated the cloth they sold. Since 1675, female corporations of couturières flourished throughout France. They had

to contend with certain male corporations of tailors who had for
years kept female dressmakers from producing anything but undergarments. Most couturières reached some agreement with the tailors
during the eighteenth century, but unhappily, the growing number
of male dressmakers and even male embroiderers[38] gave women stiff
competition.

The majority of corporations admitted workers of both sexes. A
few, such as metallurgy or tailoring men's would not accept females.
But working women were in evidence everywhere. They (especially
widows exercising their late husbands' trade) could aspire to master-
ship in many corporations. Naturally, women understood that working in a man's world they would usually be relegated to inferior posts
and certainly to far lower salaries. Yet despite this discrimination,
on those rare occasions when female workers attempted to strike,
they did so not for the female cause but for their ill-paid men as well.

When it came to political action, women had, theoretically, an
age-old right giving them a voice in public affairs. Since the Middle
Ages they were permitted to attend city and village meetings of town
assemblies, meetings in which all manner of community problems
were discussed and resolved. Still, although this right still existed in
the eighteenth century, for some reason it was no longer exercised.
Such lack of participation does not mean, however, that the women
kept their peace. In Toulouse, Caen, Rouen and elsewhere the rising
prices of grain, cotton and other commodities had peasant women
rioting in the streets at various moments of the century. And in Les
Halles, the "belly of Paris," female food vendors could cause a
nuisance as no others could. Loyalists in pre-Revolutionary times,
emotionally tied to King and court, these women harbored, nonetheless, bomb-proof opinions on certain political events. They opposed
the peace of Aix-la-Chapelle in 1748; they protested the replacement
of the Paris Parlement by a royal chamber in 1753. Before the
Revolution their complaints did not take the form of truly organized
demonstrations. They erupted rather in spontaneous explosions provoked by a street quarrel or the mere mention of an unpopular
political figure.

Once the revolutionary whirlpool engulfed France, however, it
was another story. On Monday, October 5, 1789, many Paris bakers
had no bread to sell. This was catastrophic, since, at that time, bread

was the main staple of the lower-class diet: workers and peasants required two to three pounds per person every day. They suspected that government authorities and grain dealers were encouraging a famine for their own profit. At 8:00 a.m. that day, women from Les Halles and the Faubourg Saint-Antoine gathered in front of the Hôtel de Ville which they pillaged for arms, and they asked a man called Maillard to lead them in a march to Versailles. On their way, they recruited other women or forced them to join, and several thousand angry females paraded to the court, plundering shops along the way. Madame de la Tour du Pin tells how an advance guard of 300 to 400 of them arrived while Louis XVI was out hunting, broke into the Assembly Chamber, where, drunk and exhausted from their march, they took possession of the benches and rostrums. They entered the palace too and got as far as the anteroom of the Queen's apartments, then later made their way to town and the wineshops. Soaked through from the rain, they slept in stables and coach houses.

> Those who had invaded the ministry ate everything they could find and then went to sleep on the floor of the kitchens. Many of them wept, saying that they had been forced to march and that they did not know why they were there.[39]

What had begun as a concerted, ominous manifestation from a large female pressure group disintegrated into a haphazard, pointless wandering of a swarming horde. A few leaders made their demands, using Monsieur Maillard as their spokesman, and Lafayette dreamed up some appeasing words for the group. The historian Georges Lefebvre has said, "the intervention of the women had accomplished nothing."[40] Still, as sordid and nightmarish as it seemed and as fruitless as it, indeed, proved, this demonstration of women was, nevertheless, a political event and a stirring, awesome one.

Sporadically, other collective demonstrations of lower-class women took place in Paris and the provinces, especially during the last years of the century. And, as we shall see (Chapter 5), it was in those post-revolutionary years too that certain women of the lower classes would enter the political arena as women, demanding new rights for their sex.

* * * * *

In surveying the whole sociological cross-section of women in eighteenth-century France, we may ask ourselves what discoveries we have made concerning feminine liberty and power. The answer seems to take the form of a patchwork quilt in which pieces of one design alternate with portions of others to form a picture of fragmented irregularity within an overall structure of apparent harmony. Although the population can be divided into the neat trinity of upper, middle and lower classes, and although the latter part of the century gave women some advantages they had lacked, we can discern no logical pattern such as a steadily increasing or decreasing amount of freedom, equality or prestige from one end of the spectrum to the other. Instead, we perceive a strange series of contradictions and contrasts at each level of female society.

In the case of the highest echelon of court nobles and their upper bourgeois imitators, we find a young girl held aloof from her family and literally sold into marriage with little and sometimes no freedom of choice. Then, conversely, once married, she is fairly free of conjugal demands, lives her own life and wields considerable power politically and economically. But with all her independence, she conforms (willingly) to the rigid and artificial rules of her society; with all her influence and power, she may be immersed in debt.

The middle or lower bourgeoise, on the other hand, is freer before marriage, has a greater say in the choice of her husband, but after the wedding lacks the autonomy and authority of the upper-class woman. She shares in her husband's work, even to the extent of being his partner or associate, but at the same time she is considered his subordinate. And she is bound by religious belief and a traditional moral code.

The actress is adored and despised as well. She has more power than a playwright but she lives in the margin of society. The prostitute is on top of the world at the seductive courtesan level, enjoying sexual liberty and wealth; yet fear and misery are her destiny at the sordid extreme of her trade.

A lower-class female in industry may be thrown on her own as a teenager, living free from family constraint. In marriage she is every bit as active as her husband, but she earns less pay than he and, like the peasant woman, she is most often considered inferior to him.

Finally, although a female might suffer profoundly from her husband's demise, an eighteenth-century woman with more ambition than grief would not be too unwise in welcoming the state of widowhood as her lot: as we have seen, it had its compensations.

This disparate list of feminine pluses and minuses may be informative, but it is naturally disconcerting. When writers of those days considered paradoxical facts such as these, they reached totally different conclusions. Reactionaries were enraged that women had become such a dominant force in society. Liberals were indignant that women were oppressed by that same society. Both set about proving their point by asking the same question: "What is Woman?"

A Woman of the People: "La Maraichère" (David)

2

Polemics and Propaganda

What is Woman? For centuries writers had raised the question, and for centuries some answered that she was everything and others nothing. In 1776 an anonymous tongue-in-cheek comment on the big question carried the title, "Paradox on Women, in Which the Author Attempts to Prove that They Are Not of the Human Species."[1] Earlier, another unnamed Frenchman, author of a "Controversy on Women's Soul," had announced quite seriously that "Woman, [who is] created solely for man, will cease to exist at the end of the world, because she will cease to be useful to the object for which she was created, from which it follows necessarily that her soul is not immortal."[2] (Small wonder that these authors wanted to remain anonymous!) But certainly, in the Age of Enlightenment, few philosophers held or dared to utter such unpopular opinions. Indeed, most of them were quite willing to put the souls of women (and even animals) on a par with those of men. If eighteenth-century writers discussed the what-is-woman problem at all, it was in order to tackle a more immediate question, that is: what *should* she be? How many people in pre-revolutionary France were prepared to answer "Everything"?

Oddly enough, despite the liberal atmosphere of the Enlightenment, a good feminist was hard to find. This lack is especially surprising, since, from 1753 on, quite a few sincere and eloquent writers did attempt to make woman's cause their own. They fell short of their mark, however, and for two main reasons: their writings either suffered from a naïve, puerile brand of argumentation or foundered in an ambivalent (and consequently conservative) view of woman's role. Not until the 1790's and Condorcet did eighteenth-century France discover a vigorous champion of "le beau sexe."

The last feminist worthy of the name had been the seventeenth-century writer Poulain de la Barre. With a methodical logic reminiscent of his idol Descartes, Poulain had stated that women were as suited as men for business, theology, medicine, science and law, and that they should be given the chance to prove it. Now eighteenth-century defenders of woman's cause were more than happy to discuss the issues. They wrote at length about woman's freedom, her equality or inequality in a man's world, her image and her behavior, her mind and her education, her role in marriage and her right to divorce. But—alas!—most of their literature was cold hash after the sizzling steak of a Poulain de la Barre.

A few strong voices did make themselves heard. Writers like Philippe-Florent de Puisieux,[3] the Chevalier de Jaucourt,[4] the Baron d'Holbach[5] and Boudier de Villemert[6] stand out above the rest. These men attacked custom, prejudice, education and the law for tying woman's hands in many spheres, and they decried woman's domestic bondage which they termed "slavery." Holbach protested the lack of a decent education for females and the forced marriages which encouraged unloved and unloving women down the path of infidelity. Boudier de Villemert condemned the frivolous image assigned to females and their traditional role of pleasing men. The Marquis de Puisieux pointed out very rationally that centuries of habit had unjustly excluded women from public affairs, theology and other "masculine" realms. Of these four, the liberal Chevalier de Jaucourt had undoubtedly the largest reading public for his sympathetic commentary, since he authored most of the article "Woman" in the celebrated eighteenth-century *Encyclopédie.*

Throughout this article, Jaucourt demonstrates an unusual open-mindedness on the subject of women. The main thrust of his thesis is woman's right to divorce; but while making his points he poses some intriguing questions and makes some resounding statements concerning sexual equality. Like Puisieux, Diderot and others, Jaucourt underlines the great resemblance between man and woman: he muses, Could woman be an imperfect man?[7] But rather than continue in this biological vein, he speaks of her current plight vis-à-vis man and marriage. Woman is held in domestic bondage, he writes. Yet she does not have the right to divorce. Religion is the villain here: Judaism considered women on a lower level than men; Christianity allowed females some consideration only out of pity for their weakness and inferiority. Actually, however, says Jaucourt, it is impossible to prove that a husband's authority derives from any natural male superiority. Such an idea clearly negates the modern belief in natural equality. Conclusion: Subordination of females in marriage is not the result of *natural* but of *civil* law, and nothing prevents society from changing this civil law. By its very nature, marriage is a contract. Ergo, its rights may be *reciprocal.*

Unfortunately, few of Jaucourt's contemporaries could match him in promoting the feminist cause. If we examine some of the apologies for women that they did turn out, we find their arguments arbitrary, archaic or extravagant and usually poorly presented, in short, self-defeating. Take the Jesuit priest Caffiaux. In his *Defense of the Fair Sex*[8] he appears convincing enough when he repeats the logical arguments and phrases of Poulain de la Barre, but then he insists on ruining his case by naïvely attempting to prove the unprovable: that Eve was superior to Adam, that women are more religious than men, less ambitious, more in command of their emotions; that they are submissive, charitable, sweet, complaisant, polite and a good influence overall. Although Puisieux's work is far more coherent than Caffiaux's, he too stretches his point a bit when he explains that women would make fine soldiers, since the Amazons and Joan of Arc proved so outstanding on the battlefield!

Writers who were more sophisticated than Caffiaux, those who knew how to enunciate reasonable arguments articulately, simply did not go far enough. Each one appeared to have doubts in one area or another about the role and capacity of females. And for each, the ideals of feminine liberty and equality were qualified and weakened in the light of age-old concepts of the essence or "nature" of females. Hence we have a whole string of would-be feminist brochures that appear incendiary at the outset but that soon fizzle out like a wet bonfire. Let us glance at a few of these.

One of several books entitled *Woman's Friend*[9] speaks strongly in favor of a wife's right to divorce. A reader might expect new and progressive ideas from the author, Boudier de Villemert. He goes on to say, however, that parents should continue to arrange marriages without their daughter's consent, for they are far better qualified than she to find her a rich and respectable husband. As for a young fiancée, her main contributions to the union should be her beauty and her sweet complaisance. So much for Boudier de Villemert.

In his *Essay on Women*[10] Antoine-Léonard Thomas offers readers a whole history of female accomplishments from antiquity to his time. He ends by exhorting women to abandon superficiality and fickleness and to become more solid, substantial creatures. Yet Thomas has his reservations, and considerable ones at that: women cannot expect to triumph in the arts, in philosophy or in politics. They are incapable of patriotism since they prize their men above their nation; they cannot be equitable, for their emotions lead them either into an excess of pity or an excess of vengeance. Obviously, Thomas' erudite tribute to women does precious little to advance their cause.

Can we expect better from the second-rate playwright Desmahis? After all, he, like Jaucourt, provided some pages on women for the *Encyclopédie*. His article seems promising at first glance. He offers us a witty satire of a young lady's shallow upbringing and exposes the artificiality of the role she plays. But by modern standards Desmahis would surely be labelled "male chauvinist." His curious analysis of woman's nature will bear this out. Woman's mind, opines Desmahis, is less capable of attention than a man's "because of the delicacy of [her] organs."[11] She perceives faster but focuses on ideas for a shorter period of time. She is vindictive (out of weakness), curious and indiscreet. But lest Desmahis offend any female readers by such observations, he hastens to add that the two sexes are really nearly equal in the qualities they possess. Basically, they each have as many fine traits, for one can list four on each side. Man has 1) Strength, 2) Majesty, 3) Courage and 4) Reason. Woman has 1) Grace, 2) Beauty, 3) Finesse and 4) Sentiment. We shall leave this fine philosopher with no further comment!

When it came to better known *philosophes* like Diderot, Montesquieu or the Abbé de Saint-Pierre, they all deplored what they called man's tyranny over woman, and at times they lavished tribute on the fair sex. But their praise was most often of a gallant, flirtatious variety. When Saint-Pierre composed a letter on women for the eyes of Madame Dupin, he filled it with exaggerated praise and wild assertions that nullified all of his affirmations on behalf of the feminine potential. Yes, wrote the Abbé, we men keep you down, but that's because we're afraid you'll surpass us. If you were the lawmakers, your sweetness would improve our legislation. Your lack of violence makes this a better world, and so on. The author also considers with some delectation the possibility of watching female warriors fight naked, and he suggests that males might even become *Hausfrauen.* But this bit of Saint-Pierre whimsey is hardly convincing.

Inevitably, these writers, like the lesser known polemicists, continue to view woman as another kind of animal. Occasionally this may work to the advantage of females. In his *Essay on Women,* for example, Denis Diderot offers the backhanded compliment, "When they have talent I think it is of a more original stamp than our own."[12] But even pitiful reassurances such as this are rare. Throughout his essay Diderot theorizes about essential qualities of women. They have a more mobile mind than men and more delicate organs. They lack natural or acquired strength of character (Diderot does blame this on their neglected education). And at one point a marvelling Diderot exclaims, "Oh women, you are certainly extraordinary children!"[14] This article on women was intended as an improvement over Thomas' essay on the subject. What Diderot reproached in Thomas was that he just didn't seem to *like* women enough: his work lacked sentiment. Now Diderot's own article had sentiment enough for both writers,[15] but a modern woman's reaction on reading it would assuredly be "Don't do us any favors, Denis!"

It was the political scientist Montesquieu who made "natural" a big word in France through his theories on natural law—and Montesquieu had the knack of interpreting "nature" to suit his own opinions. Out of his rather arbitrary concept of woman's *nature* he made some rather arbitrary pronouncements on what the law should and should not grant her. For example, on the side of liberation, he favored divorce (although not out of sympathy for wives), and he opposed certain laws that oppressed women, such as Henry the

Eighth's edict that an adulterous female should declare her sin to the King. On the other hand, Montesquieu agreed with legislators that daughters should be excluded from the right of inheritance. And he contributed the following to the collection of eighteenth-century essentialistic declarations on the weak sex: "Nature, which distinguished men [from women] through their strength and reason. . . gave beauty to women and intended their influence to end with that."[16]

And so this shopworn melody reverberated to some extent or another in the most liberal feminist apologies of the day. Even the progressive Holbach referred at one point in his writing to "Women, whom nature has rendered generally more sensitive, weaker and therefore more subject to anger than men."[17] And Boudier de Villemert stated, "I believe that it suits women to stay somewhat in the background."[18] After all, he said, wasn't their role to communicate their sweetness to men and to refine society?

Were the literary authors of the day any more forward-thinking than these polemicists? As a matter of fact, not many literary authors bothered to discuss woman's liberty or equality in their works. Three can be found, however, in the realm of the theatre: Nivelle de la Chaussée, Marivaux and Beaumarchais. Known in France as the inventor of "tearful comedy," Nivelle de la Chaussée regaled husbands and wives with a dramatic condemnation of the nobleman's fashionable prejudices against conjugal bliss. The heroine of *The Stylish Prejudice,* a faithful wife whom the author has ingeniously named Constance, bears her husband's indifference stoically during five full acts, only to find that a mysterious suitor who has been showering her with unwanted presents is actually—yes, that's it—is actually her very own husband. Between mistresses he happened to discover that he was madly in love with his dear wife. Naturally, not wanting to appear ridiculous, he hid the good news from her. But now circumstances force him into the open, and voilà, there he is in the last scene on his knees before his good woman and declaring his passion openly. So the female victim had her champion in Nivelle de la Chaussée, at least insofar as the "stylish prejudice" was concerned. Yet we cannot consider him truly radical or progressive. His play was a pure case of opportunism: he anticipated the coming sentimental trend in drama and knew how to wrench tears from his audiences. Beyond that, no more need be said of him here.

Marivaux seems to have gone somewhat farther than Nivelle. In *The Game of Love and Chance,* the heroine's sympathetic bourgeois father, unlike the autocratic paternal villains of Molière, grants his daughter the freedom she wishes to observe her fiancé closely before accepting him in marriage. Even more significant than this, another play, *The Colony*, appears to offer a true feminist manifesto to audience and readers. In a Lysistrata-like strategem, the women in a new island community revolt against their men. They are determined to make themselves unattractive to all males until they can have equal rights and a say in formulating the laws of their colony. Says one of their leaders

> Here are my words: you will be on a par with men; they will be your comrades and not your masters. Everywhere Madame will be worth just as much as Monsieur or I'll die in the effort.[19]

We begin to be optimistic, but wait—at the end of the play this militant speaker, Madame Sorbin, turns out in reality to be an ignoble character disdained by men and women alike. Then, in the last scene, a *deus ex machina* intervenes in the guise of a horde of invading savages. Naturally, since males are stronger, the women have to give up their little revolution and turn to their men for protection. Finally, a male protagonist assures the ladies that after the war their wishes will be considered in the laws to be made (by men, of course!) It would never have occurred to Marivaux to let one of his heroines be anything but the epitome of feminity, coquetry and gracious charm. He loved to capture them in the first embarrassed flutterings of love or in moments of transparent feminine artifice. He smiled at them sympathetically and made audiences smile at the dear, amusing creatures too. This is hardly the attitude of a progressive feminist, to be sure. It is, on the other hand, the attitude of one of the most typical of eighteenth-century writers—Marivaux.

What a difference between the dainty musings of a Marivaux and the call to arms of a Beaumarchais. France was almost in the throes of its Revolution when Beaumarchais offered his readers a true and convincing plea for women's rights. In his *Marriage of Figaro,* an unwed mother, Marceline, launches a bitter diatribe against society and its male lawmakers:

Marceline (heatedly): Men, ungrateful men, who disdainfully tear to shreds the playthings of your passions, your victims! It is you who should be punished for our youthful errors, you and your magistrates, so enamored of the right to judge us; you who out of guilty negligence allow us to be deprived of every honest means of subsistence. Is there any way at all for miserable girls to make a living? We had a natural right to women's fashions. But now you let a thousand workers of the opposite sex into the field.

Figaro (angry): They even let soldiers do embroidery now!

Marceline (carried away): And women of higher ranks receive only superficial consideration from you. Deceived by an apparent respect, kept in actual servitude; treated as minors for our possessions, punished as adults for our faults. Oh, in every respect your behavior toward us fills us with horror, or pity![20]

Here is one of the strongest feminist statements of the era. Yet the actors of the Comédie-Française deleted it and most of this scene from the actual stage production, believing that the seriousness of the tone and subject would drag their lively play down. Was Beaumarchais the great liberationist of the day? Once again, the answer is no. Although at times he liked to fancy himself woman's kind protector, in theory and in his personal life he was anything but consistent in his attitudes toward women and their rights.

By this time the reader may have become aware that almost all arguments listed here have sprung from the pen of male writers.[21] Were women utterly silent? Not entirely. Madame de Lambert, Madame de Graffigny, Madame Riccoboni and others wrote encouraging words about the talents and capacities of females. Even in the relatively non-polemic first half of the century women like Mademoiselle Archambault (in 1734) and Madame Galien (in 1737) composed well-documented apologies of their sex. But by and large such efforts had even less impact than the male output. They were timid ventures with very little bite to them. All of Mademoiselle Archambault's erudite proofs, for example, were aimed at demonstrating that women were more faithful than men. We find the same sort of anticlimactic demonstration in *How We Ought to Regard Women,* written by Madame de Coicy in 1787, just before the outbreak of the Revolution. In this pamphlet, Madame de Coicy proved

Si l'on veut jetter les —
yeux sur touttes les relations
des Indes ou la coquetterie —
~~doit être encore bien~~ quoy que
grossiere ~~en plusieurs lieux~~
non est & + naturelle
~~par raport à nos idées~~ —
on verra les h peints, —
non seulement de rouge
mais de touttes couleurs.
On leur verra les oreilles
le nés; les Levres percées
pour y passer des pierres,
de petittes écailles d'animaux
brillans et le front tailladé

Fragment of Madame Dupin's Writings on Women

to her satisfaction that there was little difference between the sexes outside of their sex, but she used all her eloquence, energy and ink merely to convince men that their honorary decorations should be shared with their wives.

A distinguished lady of French society gave long hours to drafting a promising (but incompleted) work in defense of woman. Madame Dupin de Francueil, an illegitimate daughter of the banker Samuel Bernard (and later grandmother of George Sand), became incensed upon reading certain passages of Montesquieu's *Spirit of the Laws,* passages in which the political scientist showed himself to be vastly unfair to the fair sex. So Madame Dupin asked her secretary to help her draw up a well-documented refutation of Montesquieu, in defense of womankind. Now it happened that her secretary at the time was a young man named Jean-Jacques Rousseau, the same Jean-Jacques who would later declare that woman's only function was to serve man. But whether or not Madame Dupin's feminist assignment bothered Rousseau, he dutifully set about writing down the notes that Madame Dupin had researched with his help.[22] These unpublished notes[23] contained some ardent statements on the subjects of sexual equality. Madame Dupin may have put too much effort into anthropological sleuthing that provided her with the unrevolutionary argument that, like women, primitive men enjoyed painting their faces and wearing earrings. Nevertheless she attacked firmly and directly Montesquieu's contention that masculine inheritance was "natural," and she argued vehemently against any official endorsement of woman's subservience to man.

Had Madame Dupin lived in another age, she might have polished off her work and thrown the grenade where it would have hit hardest and loudest. But her unvoiced indignation had literally no public and no consequences. Indeed, few other women even got as far as she did—to the angry note-taking stage.

Like men, most women of that time simply did not think in terms of sexual equality. Any reflecting that Madame de Lambert, Madame de Genlis or others did on the subject stopped short at the point where woman's nature, woman's place and woman's modesty formed a stone wall, reminding them relentlessly that women should be women. Not until the Revolution did women's voices ring out for their cause: until then it was up to the men. And we have seen repeatedly that although these male advocates may have been liberal by eighteenth-century standards, they still thought of women in eighteenth-century terms.

Then suddenly, as the century pushed on to an end, the subject went from simmer to full boil. Rousseau touched off a whole series of arguments with his reactionary statements on his ideal of a super-feminine-woman-submissive-to-man, Restif de la Bretonne, familiarly dubbed "the gutter Rousseau" ("le Rousseau du ruisseau"), came out with his *Gynographes* in 1776 and gave it the ample subtitle, "Project for Regulations Proposed to All Europe, to Put Women Back in their Place and by Such Means Work Efficiently toward the Reform of Morals." Little more is needed to tell us where Restif stands, but a browser curious enough to open his book can learn that "since women are to be in a different position from men all their lives, their upbringing should be absolutely different." According to Restif, they should be bound up as babies, and each of them should understand from her childhood days on that she is destined for man, "the sovereign chief of society."[24]

Here is an out-and-out cry for repression—repression of freedom and equality for females. We can gather from his subtitle that Restif held liberated women responsible for the low state of morals in his country. And obviously, if he wanted to put them "back in their place," it is because they were actually miles away from the sweet and submissive role he was anxious to give them.

By the late 1770's, women had become so active and vociferous in politics that on the eve of Revolution male counterattacks in the form of a barrage of angry pamphlets swept their way with a vengeance, assailing them with a wide variety of complaints. For example, an anonymous *Advice to Ladies,* printed in 1788,[25] accuses women of "political idiocy," and insists that their raging republicanism stems from a deepseated resentment against their own husbands. According to this writer, women furiously undermine the State instead of attacking the real objects of their anger. They don't want the King to be obeyed but they insist on being obeyed themselves.

Around a year earlier, a certain Chevalier de Feucher launched his own offensive against French females, blaming them entirely for the corruption of morals in their society. This document provoked Madame Gacon Dufour into writing a pamphlet *For the Feminine*

Sex Against the Masculine Sex (Mémoire pour le sexe féminin contre le sexe masculin) in 1787.[26] Madame Gacon Dufour wanted to make it clear that Feucher's charge did not hold water, and she offered some rather ingenuous examples to prove it: examples of female modesty, courage, charity and sensitivity! But she did score some valid points when she reminded Feucher of the injustice of forced marriages and of the fact that a woman past her prime and left on the shelf was in a sorry position in their society. She concluded her essay by surmising that no matter where you put the blame, the eighteenth century was undoubtedly no more corrupt than the seventeenth.

Counterattacks like Madame Gacon Dufour's must have only encouraged the flood of pamphlets against women. Of these brochures, the ones that enjoyed the greatest vogue were certain tongue-in-cheek satires that mixed sex and revolution. Not all of these could truly be called antifeminist, since they didn't all really deal with sexual equality. But they certainly helped to keep the female quarrel alive. 1788, for example, saw the publication of the *Very Serious Remonstrances of the Palais-Royal Girls to Messieurs Nobles,*[27] an anti-aristocratic tract. In this anonymous brochure, undoubtedly written by a man, we find the republican Palais-Royal prostitutes attacking the nobles for their hostility to the lower classes. The girls' main message to these nobles:

> If you persist in your anti-democratic attitude, our doors will be closed to you, you will experience palpitations of despair, the embraces of sorrow and pain and the convulsions of death. We alone will be the cause of that and we'll faint from pleasure.[28]

One of the most outrageous of these satires is the *Official Report and Protest of the Most Numerous Order of the Realm, the C. . .* (1789). The abbreviation "C. . . ," as any good Frenchman knows, would stand in this instance for *cocu* or cuckold. What does that have to do with protest and politics? The author of the tract explains:

> At a moment when all France resounds with cries for liberty, for a constitution, for patriotism; when every order defends its respective rights and when the tiniest corporation submits its wishes to the tribunal of opinion, the Most Numerous Order of the Realm will not remain silent. . .[29]

So these cuckolds (all referred to by initials but clearly recognizable to eighteenth-century readers) have drawn up their bill of rights, and the rights are actually lists of female wrongs. *Item:* "Every blue stocking who imagines herself an authoress will be condemned by society to return to her knitting."[30] *Item:* Dowries will be abolished, "in order to make women less capricious, vaporous, imperious, crochety, lazy, spendthrift. . ."[31] Needless to say, this publication did not go unnoticed and unanswered. The same year Paris was favored with the *Answer of the Women of Paris to the Report of the Most Numerous Order of the Realm.*[32] This was a gravely indignant sermon directed to the author of that bit of slander. What right did he have to accuse women of such treachery? It was lamentable, dangerous libel. The idea of publishing a list of cuckolds like that! That was unjust defamation, good only for disturbing the public peace. Was this piece written by some respectable and wrought-up lady? Léon Abensour thinks not, and he attributes it instead to some further misogynistic horseplay. In any case the shower of brochures for and against women continued to inundate France in 1789 and during the decade that followed. The male offensive came out more often than not with the sly brand of raillery seen in the pamphlets we have just quoted. The few women who tried to make a case did so in dead seriousness. Their attempts had the impact of so many toy balloons.

Then, finally, when the Revolution went into full swing, France heard several female voices demanding female rights and demanding them in a tone of authority. Just as peasants and artisans became conscious of themselves as a class during the revolutionary period, some women too began to think of themselves as part of a group that was being denied its rights. Olympe de Gouges was one of these feminists. In 1791, she drafted a *Declaration of Woman's Rights* which underlined the important role women should play in political assemblies and in the life of the French nation. It was Olympe de Gouges who declared so flamboyantly: "Women surely have the right to step up to the political rostrum, since they have the right to step up to the scaffold." In 1793, the actress Claire ("Rose") Lacombe, known less for her words than her deeds, forced her way into a meeting of the General Council, much to the horror of the men who had been holding forth there.

This new feminist spirit, born of the Revolution, is captured in an anonymous document, *Women's Request of the Assembly of Notables for Admission into the States-General.* It reads:

> You have destroyed all ancient prejudices, but you do nothing about the most ancient and most universal one, the one which withholds position and honor and, above all, the right to sit among you, from one-half of the inhabitants of the realm. . . You have broken the scepter of despotism. . . yet every day you allow thirteen million slaves to wear the chains of thirteen million despots! . . .[33]

Although some women did speak up forcefully in those revolutionary days, their voices were heard only rarely. Moreover, the most outstanding, the most rational and convincing plea for women's rights came from a man, the Marquis de Condorcet. In his *Essay on the Admission of Women to Citzenship*[34] Condorcet reminded his readers that when our natural rights are violated over a long period of time, habit makes us so familiar with this injustice that we don't even dream of protesting. Here we have one-half of the population excluded from rights of citizenship; yet it would be difficult to prove that women are incapable of possessing these rights. Yes, they do have periods and they become pregnant, but don't men get gout and bad colds?

Then one by one Condorcet went at all the antifeminist arguments of the day. *Males are naturally superior to females?* It is true, wrote Condorcet, that women have not been notorious for making great discoveries in science [where were you when we needed you, Madame Curie?], and perhaps there are no true female geniuses in arts and letters. But even if you admitted all this, is every male citizen a genius? *Women are not suited to politics? Female rulers could be influenced by their lovers?* Condorcet cited the two outstanding examples of great women rulers in modern history, England's Elizabeth I and Catherine II of Russia. If they had lovers, these men were surely no more powerful or dangerous than famous mistresses of kings. *If women had the right to vote, they might soon neglect their household commitments?* But surely, said Condorcet, peasant laborers do not forsake their ploughs and farms. And Condorcet continued to shoot holes through all the traditional objections to sexual equality. He ended by predicting (rightly) that if women had the same rights as men, chivalry would probably lose ground, but he assured his readers that domestic life and morals would only profit from such equality.

As brilliant a champion as Condorcet was, he did not have the last word. The fight continued, and for years angry ink spattered in both directions. The steady flow of vehement diatribes against emancipated women is proof enough that the feminine gender was making itself seen and heard and leaving its imprint on France of the eighteenth century.

VOLTAIRE AND ROUSSEAU

Woman is made specifically to please man.[35] (Jean-Jacques Rousseau)

In our days a woman can really be a philosopher.[36] (François-Marie Arouet de Voltaire)

It would seem only natural that, on the subject of women Voltaire and Rousseau should shake fists at each other from opposite sides of the question. On the one hand, there was Voltaire, at ease with females, cohabitating for years with a high-powered lady physicist (Madame du Châtelet) and constantly encouraging women to intellectual and creative achievement. On the other we have Jean-Jacques, ineffectual and gauche with the opposite sex, taking a simple, ignorant girl (Thérèse Levasseur) as his own life's companion and bequeathing to our modern sisters such galling statements as the one quoted above. The distance between their two viewpoints on women was emphasized by Voltaire in some impudent remarks on Rousseau's epistolary novel *La Nouvelle Héloïse,*[37] and eight years later, in an epistle to the writer La Harpe, he mocked Jean-Jacques again for preferring a rustic "fat Swiss miss" like his heroine Julie to the more aggressive Parisian women of his day.[38]

But in spite of Voltaire's raillery, and in spite of the great contrast in style and temperament between the two *philosophes,* the difference between their ideas on women is not so clear cut or absolute as one might expect. Indeed, at times their views may run parallel or even converge. Before examining these views, let us mention that the theme of women is developed to a far greater extent by Rousseau.

Voltaire and Rousseau: An Imaginary Fist Fight

Unlike Voltaire, Rousseau has elaborated on his concept of female education. Unlike Voltaire, he has offered us a detailed presentation of young ladies like Julie of *La Nouvelle Héloïse* or Sophie of his famous treatise on education, *Emile*. And, successful or not, Rousseau was aiming for some degree of psychological realism in his feminine portraits. Voltaire, on the other hand, rarely spent the time and effort to offer readers of his novels and plays female characters other than the two-dimensional variety. Moreover, any long, subjective sermons on *le beau sexe* are almost exclusively the domain of Rousseau. Yet both of these writers did comment at length on women. Both discussed their real and their ideal role in society. With both of them actual and factual accounts of women alternated with moral generalizations about them (the most "moral" of the two writers being the grandiloquent Rousseau). And for Voltaire and Rousseau, woman inevitably came into focus as the Other, as an object viewed by the male subject. No matter how important her role, it was, to some extent, relative to man. How then did Voltaire and Rousseau understand this contingent feminine role? And what, in particular, were their opinions on the real and ideal power of women and on the question of sexual equality?

Neither Voltaire nor Rousseau underestimated the power of the eighteenth-century Frenchwoman. They both understood the enormous influence of financiers' wives, salon directors, kings' mistresses, and they knew that the surest way for a man to arrive economically and professionally was through the good offices of a liberated, string-pulling, upper-class woman of the world. If we judged Voltaire's opinions solely from his satirical novels, we would find women viewed as a force for good and a force for evil. In the first category are the ladies of Parisian high society who take lovers like pills but spend their days lobbying in their husbands' interest. In the second group are those who serve as a trap. The novel *Candide* has examples enough of these: young Paquette who communicates the disease of love to the philosopher Pangloss; a Parisian adventuress who slyly relieves Candide of his diamonds; even the heroine Cunégonde, who serves unwittingly as the original sin that severs Candide from his Westphalian paradise.

But in reality, Voltaire saw the impact of women on his society as a beneficial one. In the second preface written for his tragedy *Zaïre,* he applauded the refinement that the fair sex brought to French mores, and he claimed elsewhere that without women there would be "no salvation in any domain."[39] Voltaire himself could have pointed to the extraordinary amount of time and energy that his Emilie du Châtelet put into working, or more often intriguing, in his own interests.

As for Rousseau, he wrote in *La Nouvelle Héloïse* of the healthy effect on philosophers and scientists of women who forced them to express themselves in a coherent and appealing way. Like Voltaire, Rousseau knew what it was to be sponsored by rich and prestigious Frenchwomen of his day. And the two *philosophes* did not restrict their appreciation of feminine force to their own time and milieu: Voltaire in his Piccini notebooks, Rousseau in his *Emile,* listed wars and revolutions ignited or inspired by women. To quote Rousseau:

> Through a woman Rome achieved its liberty, through a woman the plebeians obtained the Consulate, through a woman Rome besieged was saved from the hands of an outlaw. . .[40]

But as we know, when it came to theory, Rousseau adopted the stand of the most reactionary antifeminist. It was in his fifth book of *Emile,* devoted to the education of young Sophie, that this writer made such notorious pronouncements as, "Woman is made to give in to man and even to endure his injustices."[41] And if Rousseau created Sophie in the first place, it was because, like Adam, Emile needed a mate. Throughout Sophie's education we are reminded that women are *by nature* weak, passive, gentle and shy. Now and then Rousseau confides to the reader that, in the battle of the sexes, weak woman will eventually triumph over strong man. But how? By playing from her very weakness: "Her orders are caresses, her threats are tears." And so much for Jean-Jacques' righteously lyrical antifeminism.

What a difference between theory and practice! Rousseau's own heroines never rule artfully, through sweet caresses and helpless tears. They rule triumphantly, with firmness and conviction, because that is precisely the behavior that Rousseau and his male protagonists want from them. No sooner do Emile and Sophie come to an understanding when Emile begs his loved one to do with him as she will: "to tell him what he must do, to command instead of asking, to accept instead of thanking, to stipulate the number and times of his visits. . ."[42] And Sophie quickly complies.

In skimming through the letters that make up *La Nouvelle Héloïse,* we find Julie's missives to her lover Saint-Preux replete with imperatives. Even her fourth letter, a heartfelt supplication to him, ends with the sober admonition: "You will be virtuous or hated; I will be respected or cured."[43] And in case the reasonable Julie should not feel utterly secure in her authority, Saint-Preux quickly assures her: "It is up to you to direct our destinies. . . From this moment on I give you control over my will for life; order me as you would a man who is no longer anything for himself. . ."[44] And Julie, without the hint of a hesitation, blithely takes care of the strategy, directs the *mise en scène* of their first kiss and their second tryst, advises Saint-Preux how to act with her father, sends him on trips despite his protests and gives him money, all the while dispensing such harsh words as "grovelling soul," "vulgar heart," and telling him to be a man for a change.

What is more, when Julie marries her power extends over a whole community. It is true that Wolmar, her fatherly husband, is theoretically above her, but he acts only with her consent. He may see all and know all, but he does not will all. Wolmar's delegation of authority to his wife is totally laissez faire: she is in charge. It is Julie who manages their affairs; it is she who settles quarrels, dispenses charity, raises the children, directs the landscaping and so forth. When Julie conducts Saint-Preux through a grove that she has designed, she tells him: "I am the supervisor. . . my husband leaves me entire control over it."[45]

Julie's remark has an echo in *Emile* when Rousseau explains (in his section on Sophie) that man commands but that woman must *govern* this male commander: "She must reign in her house like a minister [of] state."[46] The best household, he tells us, is the one in which the wife holds the most power (although this power must not be usurped outright). We can recognize here the language of Rousseau's *Social Contract:* Man is sovereign and woman is the executive power carrying out his will. In *La Nouvelle Héloïse* this system is immediately legitimized through a pact between the sovereign male (Wolmar) and the governing female (Julie). But when Rousseau tells us in *Emile* that a woman should govern like a minister of state, he

Saint-Preux Visits Julie de Wolmar
in *La Nouvelle Héloïse*
(Moreau the Younger)

Emile Meets Sophie
(Moreau the Younger)

adds: "By arranging it so that she is ordered to do what she wants to do."[47] This political sleight of hand clearly places will on the side of the female, or rather, sneaks it there.

The limits and scope of the executive authority were never spelled out in *The Social Contract,* but we may be sure that a household or a community governed by a Rousseau heroine could only be a benign despotism. The reason for this is that Rousseau's female characters never usurp power: they don't have to, since their males have already abdicated it. Emile is weak and reasonable. Saint-Preux is weak and emotional. Saint-Preux's will is so utterly alienated that he is prepared to be whatever Julie wishes and to perform any act she commands, even burning down the Capitol.[48]

Whether a slave of an imperious Julie or of an inflexible Sophie, a Rousseau lover is eternally on the floor, glued to the knees of his loved one. Yet with these men, as with Jean-Jacques himself, it is not a case of ensconcing women on pedestals in order to view them as goddesses rather than as equal human beings. Rousseau has explained his own urge to genuflection in his autobiographical *Confessions:* "To be at the knees of a loved one, to obey her orders, to have to ask her pardon was very sweet enjoyment for me."[49] Since he was too shy to confess his erotic craving for spankings, he writes, "I entertained [this desire] through situations that suggested the idea to me."[50] On his knees before flesh-and-blood lady loves like his Mademoiselle Goton, Madame Basile or Madame d'Houdetot, Rousseau himself is so content with this posture that when his fictional Emile gives lessons to Sophie, he insists on teaching on his knees, until it becomes too uncomfortable for both of them!

The shadow of Rousseau's first mistress, his dear "maman," Madame de Warens, looms behind the motherly character Julie. When Madame de Warens, thirteen years Rousseau's senior, proposed that Jean-Jacques become her lover, she told him to "take a week to think it over." This is Julie's peremptory tone in the postscript of a letter (No. 57)[50] to Saint-Preux, and her very words.

So we find that when Rousseau breathes fictional life into a soft and timid hypothetical female, she materializes necessarily into the domineering powerhouse of his dreams.

With Voltaire, this phenomenon seems almost reversed. Neither in his fiction nor in his life did women have the strong prerogatives that Jean-Jacques and his male characters invested them with. As far as Voltaire's fiction is concerned, we may see in his novels and short stories examples of powerful and even dangerous women, but these are found almost exclusively among the supernumeraries. The heroines of his stories are generally those innocent, blushing prototypes of the traditional novel of adventure or the sentimental novel. In Voltaire's theatre we find colorless ingenues described as "frail reeds." Queens like Mérope are worried and motherly, even the villainous Clytemnestra becomes mainly a maternal figure, while Elektra is her mother's girl, as pliable as Voltaire's sentimental heroine Nanine. On the other hand this writer's male characters, young or old, are most often strong and mature, no matter what fate does to them—even the puppet-like Candide speaks with authority at the end of his story.

As with Rousseau, we can trace this hierarchy of power back to the author's own character and temperament. A few paragraphs of any of Voltaire's letters to his first love, "Pimpette" Dunoyer, show clearly to what degree the young swain was in charge of the action, while it lasted. Madame du Châtelet may have had a profound influence on Voltaire, but unlike Madame de Warens and Julie, she did not carefully outline the path that her philosopher was to take and give him a week to think it over, nor would she dare give him orders. Moreover, since Voltaire was much more secure financially then Rousseau, he was, of course, in a better position to be the protector rather than the protected in personal dealings with the opposite sex. We cannot say that Voltaire actually illustrated Rousseau's theory of the sovereign male, but, given his own energy and power, he certainly came much closer to it than did the timorous Jean-Jacques.[51]

On the theoretical side of the Voltairian coin, however, is a belief in the advancement of women. For example, in direct contrast to Rousseau's opinions on the submission of women is Voltaire's own satire entitled, "Women, be Submissive to Your Husbands," an imaginary dialogue between the Abbé de Châteauneuf and the Maréchale de Grancey. The object of Voltaire's attack was Saint Paul and the aim of his satire was praise of an energetic Catherine the Great. The suggested moral is that Catherine's accomplishments should provide inspiration to all women.

If Rousseau did not follow Voltaire in beating the drum for women's progress, one of the main reasons was his constant fear that females would become males. His work was full of exhortations against such a sexual metamorphosis. Montesquieu, Restif de la Bretonne and Mercier, among others, similarly deplored the "male" woman of their day. Like these writers, Jean-Jacques was criticizing the Frenchwoman of high society whose eyes brazenly met yours, whose rouge disguised the fact that she had forgotten how to blush and who swore like a man. Because Rousseau so feared woman's defection from her sex, he insisted all the more on the "nature" of woman and on her place in the "natural order." Woman's destiny is motherhood; therefore her pattern is fixed. Even if she never has a baby, maternity is her essential function. Rousseau, as always, does not deal in exceptions but in generalizations and abstractions.

Voltaire never seriously worried that women would change sex. We find throughout his correspondence many masculine-gender references to Madame du Châtelet, the kind of woman who was, in his words, a real gentleman ("un honnête homme"). This was the Voltairian stamp of approval for females whom he accepted as equals. Voltaire did not balk at intellectual equality, nor did he shun competition from the opposite sex. He actively encouraged women to compete with men, and in his own spheres of endeavor—the philosophical, scientific and literary spheres. Certainly, the women of his and Rousseau's society were eternally busy writing poetry, plays, novels or treatises. The question is how, exactly, did Voltaire —and Rousseau—feel about women as thinking, creative people? To what extent did they think that women could and should be successful in the very domain of the *philosophes?*

Rousseau's ideas on the intellectual development of females might tempt a modern woman to violence. In his program of education for Sophie, the poor girl cannot enjoy Emile's physical liberty or his freedom from public opinion. Not only is she raised conventionally in a convent but she is taught to cultivate ruse rather than sincerity, learns religion early because she cannot comprehend it [!], and does without reading or writing since she won't need those skills right away. It is true that Rousseau's advice about bringing up boys can be just as disconcerting at times, especially when it comes to the negative and stoic program devised for Emile. But in the beginning of Sophie's education, the author too clearly underlines woman's traditional essence and insists too strongly on riveting her to that essence. He may protest that it is not he but women who bring girls up and that they can bring them up just as they please. He may ask, "Is it men's fault if pretty women enchant them with their coquettish ways?"[52] This will only invite the modern liberationist to slam the book shut.

But if she manages to read further, she will discover that a time comes when a girl's education must be *redirected*. At that point public opinion is no longer her guide; she must be steered toward her own inner personal conviction. Helping her to arrive at the right compromise between public opinion and personal conviction is the arbiter Reason. Then Rousseau asks the key questions: 1) Are women capable of solid reasoning? And 2) Should they be concerned with such intellectual activity? Surprisingly, he comes to some very flattering conclusions on the subject of female intelligence. But, as we might have expected, he makes a clear distinction between the masculine and feminine mind. He allows for equal but separate capacities. Woman has presence of mind, is penetrating, observant, adroit but not adept in the search for abstract and speculative truths, scientific principles and axioms or synthesis of ideas—although she can lead men to discover and formulate these ideas. She may be the best judge of man's merit, but she herself in not likely to be a genius. The very nature of woman's intelligence is determined by her function of pleasing man, and indeed, the proper study of womankind *is* man.

If woman is a creature strictly relative to man, with a mind geared to please and abet rather than to create, could Rousseau possibly answer his second question affirmatively—should a woman develop her mind? His answer is a categorical *yes*. His justification for this answer is similar to his justification for proposing a social contract to structure modern society. The reason for a political contract between the people and the state is this: although civilized society is corrupt, people cannot simply return to nature. Since such a return is impossible, the system of government outlined in Rousseau's *Contrat social* would at least be a way of improving ignoble society and protecting its members from tyranny and injustice. Similarly, on the subject of woman's education, Rousseau explains that in modern times, in civilized, corrupting big cities, a woman cannot remain in ignorance. Education can keep her from falling into wily men's clutches. But more than that, it can bring her the esteem of her beloved husband.

So after starting out by recommending two entirely different educations for Sophie and Emile, Rousseau has come full circle and now praises the household in which a man has a wife with whom he can talk—someone with the same education as he. The aim here may be man's pleasure, but the means are nonetheless woman's instruction and her intellectual development. Voltaire liked to make fun of Saint-Preux's critique of Parisian women in *La Nouvelle Héloïse* and his condemnation of their shocking, forward ways. But Voltaire never mentioned the second half of that critique, Rousseau's admiring look at these same women and his admiration of their interesting conversation, their knowledge and their mental capacities.

Where Rousseau tried to draw the line in the intellectual advancement of females was at the prospect of their going beyond men and becoming men's instructors. Saint-Preux is to instruct Julie; Emile is to teach Sophie and not the reverse. But as it actually turns out, Sophie outwits Emile and Julie instructs Saint-Preux. In all of *La Nouvelle Héloïse* there is only one letter in which Saint-Preux acts the professor and proposes some vague ideas on education. This is Letter 12, in which he also admits that all their previous lessons were aimed at consulting Julie's taste rather than enlightening it. Beyond that letter it is Julie who hands down opinions, judgments and advice. Julie is the inveterate "preacheress," and Saint-Preux calls her letters an "instruction manual."[53] We have come a long way from little Sophie and her female occupations.

As usual, the best explanation is found in Rousseau's own life and taste. He admired and gave homage to the cultivated women who surrounded him. There was his first protectress Madame de Warens, who knew literature, spoke well, sang, played the clavichord and concocted medicines (to say nothing of her activities as an adventuress, speculator and spy). There was the musical Madame de Francueil and the musical and literary Madame d'Epinay. There was Madame Dupin whose work on the merit of women he helped to prepare. There was Madame d'Houdetot who wrote verse and whose conversation enchanted him. And finally, if Rousseau had been completely content with the ignorance of his long-term mistress, Thérèse Levasseur, he would not have tried (in vain) to educate her.

Yet Rousseau has given his generation and ours the false impression that he wanted women to shun intellectual pursuits. Largely responsible for this misconception is Rousseau's constant criticism of pedantic women or those presumptuous bluestockings whose sharp and often cruel wit frightened and repelled him. We must remember that Rousseau made a distinction between a female pedant and an enlightened, intelligent woman.

As we might expect, Voltaire showed more enthusiasm than Rousseau on the subject of women's intellectual progress. His pride in a woman's mind and creativity shone especially in his tributes to Madame du Châtelet. And his correspondence reflected a genuine desire that the women he knew succeed in their efforts and a sincere satisfaction when they did so. We can imagine his disappointment when, in spite of all his enthusiasm and support, his niece Madame Denis was unable to make her third-rate farce, *La Coquette punie,* stageable. Had she done so, it would have proved his theory that "Women are capable of everything that we can do," and that "The only difference between them and ourselves is that they are more lovable."[54]

But was that the only difference? In a flattering letter to a correspondent, Marguerite Delaunay, Voltaire declared that her discussion of free will was "solid," but that in addition to its solidity it had the feminine qualities of "delicacy," "finesse" and "persuasion."[55] With all his feminism and good will, Voltaire, like Rousseau, still made the traditional distinction between masculine and feminine qualities of the mind. He was also apt to speak in terms of female sentiment or heart as opposed to male reason. And here and there we find Voltaire's liberal feminism tempered or qualified by the opinions of his day. In a famous epistle to Madame du Châtelet he holds that "It is true that a woman who abandoned her domestic duties to cultivate sciences would be condemnable in her very success."[56] In his article "Femme" in the *Questions on the Encyclopédie,* he states that men are superior to women not only in force but in mind, and he reminds us that there have been no women inventors. Here and elsewhere he emphasizes woman's weakness and docility, and he tends to see the prime function of women in society as refining customs and manners. Pascal termed human beings "thinking reeds." Although Voltaire allowed women the power of thought, he still could not eliminate entirely their timeworn frail reed image.

To what degree can we consider Voltaire and Rousseau progressive or reactionary on the subject of woman's equality and liberty? Jean-Jacques Rousseau claimed that women were exactly equal to men, except for their sex. But then he quickly made this sexual difference important enough to account for ninety per-cent of the female body and soul. In the last analysis, the bourgeois conservatism and social immobility of life as pictured in Rousseau's ideal community of Clarens in *Héloïse* are quite logically mirrored in his opinions on the opposite sex. His is, inevitably, a static view.

On the other hand, Voltaire, as we have seen, not only understood but supported the idea of sexual equality. On the subject of feminine liberty, his short dialogue, *Education of Girls,* published one year before *Emile,* offers a more advanced view than Rousseau gives us. An enlightened girl named Sophronie explains that her mother believes that girls should not be educated in convents since they don't usually live in them in later life. What is more, this progressive mother of hers believes that daughters should not be mated to strangers but should have a say in the choice of a husband. But just as there had been limits to Voltaire's appreciation of woman's intellect, there were limits too to the quality and quantity of equality and freedom that he allotted to females. In *Education of Girls,* the emancipated Sophronie tells us that had she not been destined for society, her mother would have educated her for "works that suited her sex."[57] And this is not meant ironically but accepted. If Voltaire was just as quick as Rousseau to denounce oppression and injustice, he was just as reluctant to suggest any real change in the social order.

One might ask whether Voltaire did not see examples of oppression of women. It was certain at the time that with all the freedom and power enjoyed by many Frenchwomen, their sex still suffered legal and economic injustices, obvious especially in the lower classes. Voltaire had undoubtedly read Jaucourt's article "Femme" in the *Encyclopédie* with its criticism of domestic servitude and its review of archaic laws inequitable to women. But he did not take up the cause. If he wrote in favor of divorce, for example, it was not, as Jaucourt did, for the protection or liberation of women but for the relief of both sexes. Voltaire could cheer women on to intellectual and artistic advancement, but he could never think of them in terms of socio-economic emancipation. How could he when the examples

he had before him were a Duchesse du Maine, a Mademoiselle
Clairon, a Madame de Pompadour or a Madame du Châtelet, and
when he himself described Frenchwomen of his days as:

> Helpmeets of their husbands, Queens where'er they be;
> Free without dishonor, faithful although free.[58]

As for Desmahis' complaint that women were educated to be
frivolous coquettes and unfaithful wives, Voltaire himself had complained about this in an ode on the evils of his times,[59] a poem that
could have been written by Rousseau (if Rousseau had been more
than one year old at the time). But Voltaire was only nineteen then,
and he was to accept this feminine education and its results more
quickly than his benighted hero Zadig acquiesced to Destiny. Besides, he not only tolerated but appreciated the traditionally feminine
aspects: the pompons, the diamonds and the graceful frills that went
along with his Newtonian Emilie—and other unfettered women of
her time.

In probing the attitudes of Voltaire and Rousseau on the subject
of woman's role, we discover, finally, that it was not the man with
the reputation for feminism, the open-minded, clearsighted Voltaire,
but the one known to posterity as a rank male chauvinist, that
muddled, mystical genius Rousseau, who had the audacity to suggest
a better education for "the half of the human race that governs the
other half,"[60] and who went so far as to equate an arranged marriage
with slavery.[61]

Certainly, we can no longer place these philosophers, as so many
critics have done, at completely opposite sides of the female question.
Rousseau's attitude is characterized by ambivalence, an ambivalence
that is usually based on the contradiction between his ideals and his
own personality. Voltaire's attitude is, like so many of his attitudes,
open-eyed and qualified. It would of course be unrealistic to conclude that the two *philosophes* are fundamentally in agreement.
Rousseau still lags far behind Voltaire on the question of woman's
role and woman's fate. But today's liberationists are doomed to
disappointment if they seek any real ammunition in Voltaire's camp.
For Voltaire, so completely colored by his century, was liberal and
tolerant on the subject, but not truly progressive. For the first *enlightened* pleas for women's rights since Poulain, France and the

Voltaire's Emilie, Madame du Châtelet (unidentified painting)

Bust of Rousseau (Houdon)   Bust of Voltaire (Houdon)

eighteenth-century Frenchwoman had to await the Revolution and, especially, Condorcet.

*   *   *   *   *

At dead center of the whole feminist quarrel lay the question of woman's intellectual potential. Just as Voltaire and Rousseau had to grapple with this problem, so did almost all the eighteenth-century pamphleteers who wished to stifle or encourage feminine ambitions. Nearly every one of these writers, no matter on which side of the issue his heart beat, agreed that there was some difference in the types of intellectual capacities that characterized the two sexes. Consequently, girls were not supposed to receive the same education as boys. This opinion was held not only by male conservatives like Restif de la Bretonne but by outstanding women contemporaries too. In a letter to Abbé Galiani, Madame d'Epinay declared that:

> . . . the most erudite woman can have only a superficial knowledge. I say therefore that a woman is not able, for the very reason that she is a woman, to acquire a broad enough knowledge to be useful to her sex. . .
> How many fields are closed to [women]! Everything that relates to the science of administration, to politics or commerce is forbidden them; they cannot and should not meddle in them.[62]

And Madame de Genlis, who survived the revolutionary period and who wanted women to better themselves academically, claimed that "a woman needs male backing," and that "she can only be esteemed for her quiet and spotless virtues."[63]

Arguments like these were hardly likely to encourage women to seek equality in education. Militating violently against such equality was an intense end-of-the-century reaction against bluestockings, or what Rousseau and his contemporaries called "brain bureaus" *(bureaux d'esprit)*. Many men—and women—were enraged by fashionable ladies with pretentions to literary genius, or salon directresses who made imperious judgements on the works of their author friends and enemies. Said Louis-Sébastien Mercier:

> What claim to fame has the woman who suddenly decides to make her entrance into the sanctuary of the muses and philosophy? She has ogled, bantered, simpered, made silk knots and little nothings. She has wasted

her mind in a sea of futility; she has only noticed glitter and has always been content with superficiality; she has blinded herself; yet she believes that she can judge a book as she can a pompon. Her mind's laziness prevents her from analyzing; her short supply of mental evergy does not permit her to understand the important elements of a work; her flightiness alights on some details and cannot take in the whole idea; she articulates the same way as she feels, in a vague, uncertain and ambiguous manner.[64]

The "brain bureaus" proved so infuriating that when the nineteenth century made its entrance it was greeted by Sylvain Maréchal's satirical *Project for a Law Prohibiting Women to Learn How to Read.* Maréchal, with humorous exaggeration, took his customary negative stand on intellectual progress for females and offered them instead, as the title suggests, total ignorance. Although few authors of the time would pretend to go that far, fewer would dream of proposing complete intellectual equality for the sexes. Even Choderlos de Laclos, whose *Education of Women* made a plea for women's right to freedom and a good education, ended his treatise by advising any educated young lady "never to show her knowledge to anyone except her most intimate acquaintances, and then only in confidence."[65]

Now, in the midst of all this arguing and theorizing, little girls were fast becoming women, and, for better or for worse, most of them were acquiring some manner of instruction along the way. A look into the nature of this instruction can surely help us to understand more fully the feminist and antifeminist polemic and may offer us some added insight into the life and destiny of the eighteenth-century Frenchwoman.

3

A Little Learning . . .

In the Age of Enlightenment, education did precious little to illuminate the minds of Frenchwomen. True, literacy in females rose astonishingly—in some regions as much as 100 percent during the century.[1] But from our modern vantage point, the quality of feminine instruction of that time seems pitifully inadequate. This was hardly a new development. For centuries the sciences had been accepted as a male domain, and only a minuscule minority of Frenchwomen had penetrated the realms of arts and letters. When it came to women, learning was a luxury. The upper classes alone, the nobility and rich bourgeoisie, produced those educated and cultured Frenchwomen whose names survive today. Héloïse, Aliénor d'Aquitaine, Marguerite de Navarre, Louise Labé, the Marquise de Rambouillet, Madame de Sévigné and other brilliantly accomplished females were rich or noble—usually both.

But, one might object, what about men? Surely, after the devastating wars and famines of the fifteenth century, they too remained in profound ignorance. The old saying "Food first, philosophy later" applied really to both men and women, and in the first half of the sixteenth century France still provided a mere minimum of educational opportunity to either sex. But the sexual disparity remained constant. For when the Renaissance and the Reform opened new avenues of learning to the French population, when proselytizing

Catholics and Protestants vied with each other in creating new parochial schools, when even the lower classes could learn in free church-
run institutions, the majority of females still received far less instruction than males. Rabelais may have marvelled that women and girls
were aspiring to the ranks of Minerva, but he undoubtedly had in mind a
select sampling of the well-bred, well-heeled women of his day.

On the surface the seventeenth century seemed to promise women
new educational opportunities. Young girls of all social ranks could
now receive formal instruction. Energetic members of the church,
finding that the sprinkling of Parisian secular schools for girls was
lamentably insufficient, had begun to create Catholic "teaching congregations" throughout France. The Ursuline sisters opened a girls'
school in Avignon in 1592 and another in Paris in 1612. A great
demand obviously existed for these institutions, because in the course
of the century the number of Ursuline French congregations rose to
around 325. Some girls paid no tuition at all and attended as day
students. They received a primary education consisting of religious
instruction, reading, writing, arithmetic and assorted household
skills. Richer girls boarded at school and acquired some further
education before they left.

Other religious orders imitated the Ursuline's example: the Augus-
tines, Sisters of Notre-Dame, Daughters of the Cross, Daughters of
Notre-Dame, Visitandines and Bernardines set up schools on the
same model. Still, despite this lively burgeoning of congregations, the
level of female education was abysmally low. For one thing, the
courses of study sorely lacked substance and rarely went beyond the
three R's of the Ursulines. Besides, before the end of the century,
most of these congregations had officially become convent orders
where nuns took their vows and where intellectual prowess took a
back seat to piety.

The sad state of feminine instruction at the time becomes even
clearer to us if we take stock of the insufficient number of schools,
inadequate buildings for classes, frustration of local community
quarrels, rivalry between the congregations and, above all, the sad
economic plight of France after the foreign wars waged during the
second half of the seventeenth century. Little wonder that cultured
women of that time were an even rarer commodity than during the

Renaissance. Any outstanding seventeenth-century female illuminate gleaned her knowledge as did her predecessors—not from formal schooling but from an undetermined number of private lessons.
The most aristocratic lady of the day could be close to illiterate,
having only a vague notion of writing or spelling. When Richelieu's
mother, Mademoiselle de Brèze, married the Duke of Enghien in
1641, she was shipped off to a convent at the eleventh hour to learn
to read and write. And two of the most distinguished noblewomen
of the seventeenth century left to posterity these dubious examples
of orthography:

> *Correct 17th-century French:* Il y a si longtemps que je n'ay entendu
> parler de vous.

> *Madame de Montespan to Madame de Lauzan:* Il lia sy lontant que je
> n'ay antandu parler de vous.[2]

> *Correct 17th-century French:* Il auroit perdu le sang s'il avoit pensé à
> faire réussir les bruits qui ont couru.

> *La Marquise d'Huxelles to Fouquet:* Il auroit per du le san sil avoit pencé
> à faire reusir les brui qui ont couru.[3]

The basic-level cultural immaturity of women was only encouraged by French society's confusion of female intelligence and
instruction with female pedantry. Molière's satire of French bluestockings, *Les Femmes savantes,* could make any lady with intellectual ambitions think twice about pursuing them. And as Thomas
remarked, in Louis XIV's reign women who longed to improve their
minds had to do it almost clandestinely.[4] But on the eve of the
Enlightenment, the seventeenth century took two giant steps in the
direction of progress: a book and a school. These were Fénelon's
Education of Girls, published in 1688, and Madame de Maintenon's
school for girls at Saint-Cyr founded that same year.[5]

In his work Fénelon proposed a program of study more thorough
and ambitious than any educational program for females that France
had known up to that time. On the assumption that girls would some
day marry, Fénelon thought why not make them efficient wives,
housekeepers and mothers? A good bourgeoise is useful to her husband if she knows more than the elementary rules of mathematics.

A landowner's wife should understand all about agriculture, feudal rights, taxes and so on. A noblewoman could help administer her husband's fortune if she were acquainted with laws governing contracts or wills. Mothers should be able to educate their little girls in almost any sphere. Although Fénelon hardly gave a nod to the lower-class woman in this treatise, he did lay the foundation for a practical, solid and extremely broad course of study for females.

Madame de Maintenon's boarding school at Saint-Cyr for impecunious daughters of noblemen and army officers was inspired to some extent by Fénelon, but it did not approach the rigorous level of training suggested in his work. Her main aims were to encourage humility in her students, provide them with religious instruction and equip them for a not-too-illustrious marriage match by giving them practice in household skills. At one time or another, every girl took a turn at sweeping the rooms, helping with the laundry, working on sewing, embroidery and tapestry. If this sounds onerous, let us add that Madame made sure that there was always breathing space for recreation, joyous laughter and affection.

Within the framework of this apparently modest and easygoing practical education, we discover in Saint-Cyr the best formal schooling that women could obtain in France in the late seventeenth and early eighteenth centuries. Pupils under twelve years of age, distinguished by their red ribbons, studied reading, writing, counting, grammar, catechism and Bible. The "greens," students from twelve to fourteen years took lessons in music, history, geography and mythology. Fourteen to sixteen-year-olds, the "yellows," took lessons in French, received more religious instruction and music, learned the minuet and the pavane. The oldest class, the "blues," ranging from sixteen to twenty, had further schooling in religion, music and French. Although this seems like a minimal course of study to us today, it represented an enormous improvement over what other schools offered, and the program also gave pupils a decent acquaintance with classic literature. As a matter of fact, the growing sophistication of the older girls was partly responsible for the ultimate downfall of Saint-Cyr. Enacting roles that the great Racine had written expressly for them, and doing this before Louis XIV and his royal court, had made the girls so worldly, ambitious and even cutthroat that they ended up by completely thwarting poor Madame de Maintenon's initial goals of modesty and humility.

Well after Madame de Maintenon's death in 1719, Saint-Cyr continued to be the model for all eighteenth-century convents. Each new religious congregational school for girls hastened to imitate its admired pattern of class colors, domestic training, and, more or less, its program of study.

So the convent school filled a gap. Throughout the first half of the eighteenth century it provided the nobility and wealthy bourgeoisie with a handy solution to the problem of a girl's education. It also provided an opportunity for valuable social contacts and a respectable baby sitter as well, one that kept boarding students out of their parents' hair and safely away from their hyperactive, breezy world. For many lower-class families it meant free primary instruction for their day-student daughters, a safeguard against idleness and mischief and a healthy religious atmosphere—all this in an institution that housed girls from a higher society.

But with all its blessings the convent could not satisfy everyone. It was constantly challenged and its merits eternally debated. The question "Should a girl be educated at a convent or kept at home?" lay at the heart of almost any eighteenth-century discussion about feminine instruction, and with each new generation the answer "Home" rang out more loudly. By the time of the Revolution, the convent had truly lost favor as a means of educating young girls. In order to understand this failure, let us see what the eighteenth-century convent was like at a time when it still occupied the tender years of so many young upper-class Frenchwomen.

Within the convent superstructure we find three main categories: 1) the abbeys, the richest and most important of the convents, each one directed by a prestigious abbess who was usually appointed by the King; 2) the priories, which were often subdivisions of the abbeys and administered by elected prioresses; 3) the more numerous simple convents or *monastères,* under the direction of "superiors" elected for a given period of time. Paris, as one might expect, boasted the most elegant convents and undoubtedly the most expensive ones too.[6] The poshest was the Pentemont, an abbey that charged as much as 600 francs a year for its ordinary plan of room, board and lessons and 800 a year for the *de luxe* plan. Other convents were slightly or much less expensive, but in all cases parents had to pay extra for private lessons from teachers recruited from the outside or for a private apartment and even personal maids for the more pampered daughters.

Each big Parisian convent had its own particular clientele. The Pentemont and L'Abbaye-aux-Bois attracted the most aristocratic young ladies of the country, girls who bore the grand names of Orléans or Polignac. On the other hand, financial scions sent their female offspring to the Conception on the Rue Saint-Honoré or to the Madeleine de Traisnel. The most renowned of provincial convents was Fontevrault, for it housed, from 1738 to 1750, the legitimate daughters of Louis XV. Like other important convents, this institution struck visitors as a city unto itself, a whole thriving community of nuns, boarders and servants, magnificently appointed and obviously well endowed.[7]

Madame de Maintenon's original Saint-Cyr had faded away, but the eighteenth-century convents (including the post-Maintenon Saint-Cyr) continued to cast themselves in its old mold: they adopted the same basic subject matter and put the same emphasis on religious instruction, music and the running of a household. Programs continued to be as busy and as regulated. Here is a day in the life of the Princesse de Ligne, when she was Hélène Massalska and a young "blue" *pensionnaire* at L'Abbaye-aux-Bois:[8]

Get up in the summer at 7:00 [Hélène was lucky: at the Ursulines it would have been 5:30!], in the winter at 7:30. Be in class, at the stalls, to wait for Madame de Rochechouart who comes in at 8:00.[9] Learn, as soon as she leaves, the Montpellier Catechism and repeat it aloud. At 9:00, breakfast; at 9:30, mass. At 10:00, read until 11:00. From 11:00 to 11:30, take a music lesson. From 11:30 to 12:00, drawing. From 12:00 to 1:00, take geography and history. At 1:00, lunch, then recreation until 3:00. At 3:00, writing and math, until 4:00. At 4:00, dancing lesson until 5:00; snack and recreation until 6:00. At 7:00, supper. At 9:30, to bed.[10]

One main difference between Saint-Cyr and its eighteenth-century imitators: Madame de Maintenon had chosen and trained promising young nuns (usually ex-Saint-Cyr girls who took their vows) to form her competent faculty. In the later convent schools, however, nuns had the role of mere assistants who mainly helped the girls practice their lessons in class, while the real professors—males—were visiting experts hired from outside the convent walls. Nuns of the prestigious convents often came from the highest nobility and some were known to demonstrate a surprisingly unchristian pride of birth. Hélène Massalska, speaking of the nun Madame de Torcy, reported, "We used to make fun of her great airs; we claimed that she found only in Jesus Christ a husband worthy of herself and that she was not sure if even that match wasn't a little beneath her."[11] Whether noble or bourgeoise, a convent nun-assistant was usually a former *pensionnaire* who had taken her vows instead of returning to the world outside.

Life in a convent was not all sober training and catechism, for, when least expected, jokes and pranks interrupted the serene and holy atmosphere. During the mysterious, silent hours of the night anything could happen. Didn't Hélène Massalska and her good pal Mademoiselle de Choiseul dump black ink into the holy water? We can imagine their stifled fit of giggles watching the nuns dip their dainty fingers into the murky liquid and piously anoint themselves. Fortunately for the tricksters, the nuns themselves burst into uncontrollable laughter when they saw what had happened, and the service was interrupted. Another night, the same culprits attached the bell cords with their hankerchiefs so that the morning reveille wouldn't ring and oust them from their beds. However, it took no master detective to recognize the initials on the guilty handkerchiefs.

Even a young married woman, Madame de Genlis, could not resist the chance to make innocent mischief while staying at a convent. When she spent some weeks at Origny-Sainte-Benoîte, how did she keep busy? She confesses delightedly:

> I ran through the corridors at night usually dressed as a devil with horns and a red face, and woke up the young nuns. I entered quietly into the cells of the old ones whom I knew to be deaf and plastered rouge and fake beauty marks on them without waking them up. They got up every night to go to the choir, and you can imagine their surprise when, having dressed hastily and without a mirror, they saw each other in church all bright red and beauty marked. I could easily get into all their cells since they are forbidden to lock their doors. . . .[12]

Most nuns accepted practical jokes and minor infractions of rules with a tolerant girls-will-be-girls smile. We know of some exceptions, however, cases of severe punishments that horrified Paris society.

When the seventeen-year-old Eléanore Dejean committed a misdeed in the Convent of the Conception, the nuns punished her by taking away her dog and donating it to the convent gardener (who later killed it).[13] Worse, at Fontevrault, girls who misbehaved did penance by descending all alone to pray in the cellar where dead nuns were entombed. According to Madame Campan, one of Louis XV's daughters suffered all her life from fits of panic inspired by her fear of this punishment.

Even more lugubrious, and certainly more baroque, was the case of a five-year-old child at the convent of Port-Royal in Paris. This young miss had stolen a coin worth six francs. The nuns of the convent condemned her to "hanging." Here is how they engineered her symbolic execution: they placed the culprit in a laundry basket and hoisted her by pullies until she was suspended close to the ceiling. Then they paraded under her basket chanting the De Profundis psalm for the dead, while fellow *pensionnaires* brought up the rear. One of these children, a six-year old, raised her head as she passed under the basket and called anxiously, "Are you dead?" A tiny voice wafted down: "Not yet." Thirty years later, the curious six-year old (now the Maréchale de Beauvau) ran into the little victim, a duchess at the French court. Her spontaneous greeting was "Are you dead?" Answered the duchess, predictably, "Not yet!"[14]

Happily, punishments such as these were uncommon. School-marmish rigidity in bringing up young girls was now a whole century out of style: it had given way to the more palatable eighteenth-century concept of tolerance. Now tolerance had its good points, but some critics thundered that it led to frivolity and even to unseemly carryings-on in the convent. In the liberal atmosphere of the Enlightenment, high-born *pensionnaires* emoted in private lessons given by worldly actors of the Comédie-Française; they pirouetted at balls in the parlors of convents like Port-Royal. More surprising still, the abbess of the Origny convent received male visitors in her apartment. If this were not enough to set tongues wagging, the Chief of Police and Keeper of the Seal D'Argenson had his own private apartment at La Madeleine de Traisnel.

The penetration of the mundane and the profane through convent walls had become an accepted *modus vivendi* in those days, and only a scant minority of purists and prudes complained of it. If there were protests—and there were indeed protests—against these institutions, they sprang from other causes. For instance, in the latter part of the century, French society began to realize the importance of physical education and hygiene. Concerned writers like Riballier and, especially, Madame de Miremont accused the convents of encouraging sloth and poor health in girls. No baths, cosmetics and clogged pores, dirty teeth ripe for decay—here we have some of Madame de Miremont's complaints. But she does not stop there: she condemns the improbable meal schedule too. She describes a convent, and not an unusual one, where the girls jump out of bed at dawn but don't have their first meal until 9:00 a.m. Then their lunch and dinner are crammed into the following eight or nine hours, the last meal coming at 5:00 p.m. So a stomach alternates between the two extremes of frenetic digestion or a gnawing hunger.

Madame de Miremont paints a bleak picture of hygiene in the girls' dormitory. Since only the classrooms had heat, no shivering *pensionnaire* would ever dream of opening the dormitory window. In the polluted air and suffocating stench of the community bedroom, young girls often slept with most of their clothes on, "some," our observer tells us, "to protect themselves from the cold; others out of laziness, for the pleasure of sleeping later the next morning." And she adds, "As a matter of fact, they do get awakened much too early for what they have to do."[15] Some of the girls restricted their circulation by wearing their whalebone corsets to bed, and certain nuns encouraged that practice ostensibly on the theory that a heavy corset preserved the body from possible nocturnal injuries. A good number of residents read in bed late at night by the flickering light of a dangerously combustible lamp.

But what of the convent education itself? Was it adequate and did it satisfy the public of that time? In most of these schools pupils absorbed, along with their catechism and music lessons, a little French literature and the basic rules of arithmetic. Geography took the form of a long, exotic list of places, and history was upstaged by mythology. Nuns did not make the most qualified coaches. In the first half of the century, especially, many of them had atrocious spelling, and their charges suffered naturally from their lack of background and talent. At Fontrevault, Louis XV's daughter, Madame Louise, couldn't read at age twelve.

For its day, the convent offered a not utterly disreputable program, but it represented no improvement over the quality of Madame de Maintenon's curriculum, and it could not match Saint-Cyr's diligent training for a domestic career. Observers like Mercier wondered why a convent education placed so much emphasis on gracious charm and so little on housewifely duties, why it put beauty before brains and why the dancing master played a more important role there than the reading teacher. The answer was that convents, in Paris especially, had a social orientation. The provincial counterparts, on the other hand, stressed religion. So, inevitably, pedagogical and practical preoccupations often took a second place. In educating French girls, the convents did precisely the job expected of them and certainly no more.

Some writers decried the lack of solid substance offered by the convents, but in fact, the main objection to these institutions was not pedagogical but social and psychological. The convent education, critics insisted, did not prepare young women for the dangers of French society. An unsuspecting *pensionnaire* lived in a closed world for years, then suddenly emerged from it, innocent and vulnerable, to plunge into the hornet's nest of eighteenth-century high life. There she received her "second education," her real education, and it could sometimes spell disaster. Witness the case of Laclos' naïvely sensual character, Cécile de Volanges. Fresh from the convent, she walked into the trap of her own ignorance and the artful affection of that eighteenth-century master logician, Madame de Merteuil. Deceived, seduced, exposed and ridiculed, Cécile abandoned family, friends and society to become a nun.

Here contemporaries could see the effect of leaving the care and education of young girls to mercenaries. They discovered that it was a mother's job to instruct her daughter or to see to it that others taught her, and not in an institution but right at home. That way a girl could make the transition between childhood and womanhood naturally and safely.[16]

This pro-home, anti-convent viewpoint became extremely popular in the second half of the century, and the convents fell increasingly out of favor. The *philosophes'* triumphant war against organized religion in the 1750's and 1760's undoubtedly encouraged this shift away from a parochial education. For the anticlerical, antireligious writer Diderot, a convent was a place where girls could be kept imprisoned, forced to take their final vows and even subjected to aberrant sexual advances, which he voluptuously described in his clandestine novel *La Religieuse.* Although the more conservative brothers Goncourt later relegated the notion of forced vows to the realm of fiction, it is true that the nun's vocation, like the priesthood, was the only recourse for many children born of large, respectable but impecunious families. Madame de Tencin, who found herself precisely in that situation, was one of the few nuns to succeed in breaking her vows. Others were less fortunate, and on-the-spot witnesses such as Madame de Genlis and Hélène Massalska have described real instances of their tragedies. Sentimental novels certainly exploited the theme of convent sequestration, but Diderot's fictional convent exposé—based on the actual case of a persecuted nun who could not break her vows[17]—could only be published safely well after the Revolution. Authors did not risk their hides by making such direct and shocking criticism public. Neither did they attack the catechistic content of the convent curriculum. Whether they felt involved or not in the religious aspect of the question, most of them insisted simply that a parent and a home education could do far more than a convent to make a good wife, mother and individual of the young Frenchwoman of their day.

Home as a private school? Until the end of the century, such a solution was unthinkable for daughters of the very rich or very noble. But many a bourgeoise did take her lessons without budging from her house, greeting in turn a variety of visiting teachers, all of them men. Even a petite bourgeoise of uncultured parents, Manon Phlipon (later Madame de Roland), took private lessons from a number of teachers. Her mother taught her the first elements of catechism. Friends of the family kindly pitched in and helped with this primary religious education. Then a whole series of safely old and ugly male instructors walked in and out of Manon's life: one teacher for geography, another for handwriting, a special teacher for dancing, for music, for guitar.

As with the convents, a home education laid great stress on the arts, but in the latter half of the century, when science came into vogue, many a young woman managed to supplement her formal instruction by private delving into scientific and philosophical tracts

—interspersed with a good dose of those deliciously clandestine novels of Voltaire and other under-the-counter literature that no self-respecting teacher would recommend.

We may well wonder if this home education actually prepared young women more successfully than the convent school. From the academic vantage point, the answer is more *and* less so. The depth and breadth of home instruction varied with each family, each teacher and each girl. Some ambitious bourgeois parents tried to provide their daughters with an impressively ample and eclectic education. The gifted Geneviève de Malboissière, who died at only nineteen years of age (1746-1766), was a product of rich, cultured bourgeois parents who encouraged their only child in her scholarly pursuits and creative projects. This talented girl often filled her charming letters with accounts—in Italian—of her day's instruction:

> After dinner I took my drawing lesson, finished Locke and started Spinoza. After the lesson I finished my theme and we went for a walk. . . . Yesterday, after mass, upset because I couldn't see you, I did my Spanish and Italian themes and then—admire my patience—read a philosphical tract. . . . This morning I took my Spanish and Italian lessons, read twenty-three pages of Plato, etc. . . .[18]

Geneviève de Malboissière may have spelled Robinson Crusoe "Robindson Chrusoé" but she ordered it in English, studied Epictetus in Greek and wrote and performed (at home) a good number of plays.

But in numerous other families, young ladies who may have possessed the curiosity of a Geneviève de Malboissière and her potential for creative and independent thinking learned next to nothing. In many rich families it was up to a governess in residence to build the foundation of a girl's education. Chances are that such a governess was nearly as uneducated as her charge. How did she get the job? Perhaps she had been a maid at Madame's toilette. No longer spry enough to run back and forth for powder and beauty marks or to stand up for an hour arranging her mistress' coiffure, she was relegated to the governess detail. *Voilà:* let her muddle through as best she can—and daughter too!

Some daughters managed to muddle through quite well in spite of an utter lack of direction. Stéphanie-Félicité Ducrest de Saint-Aubin,

who later became Madame de Genlis, was one of these.[19] Brought up
in a village of Burgundy, at age five she took reading lessons from
the village instructress and learned a little catechism and a lot of
ghost stories from her mother's maids. When she was seven an
organist's daughter taught her music and served generally as her
governess. This uncultured, untutored adolescent read the child
some more catechism, attempted a little history and, bored with it,
switched to sentimental novels and plays.

Both of Stéphanie-Félicité's parents were educated and talented;
neither of them consciously did a thing to help form their daughter's
mind. The father concerned himself with making "a strong woman"
out of her. With that goal in mind, he had the poor girl touch spiders,
toads and mice, so that she wouldn't be squeamish in later life. Her
mother, a poet of sorts, had the child take roles in comic operas of
her invention and in Voltaire's tragedies which she staged in her
home. At eight years of age, Stéphanie-Félicité charmed everyone,
including herself, in the role of Love. Her parents allowed her to
wear her cupid's costume for two years, although for Sunday mass
she was minus wings and covered with a brown cape. Later they
dressed her as a boy, and a dancing master gave her fencing lessons.
Still only eight, she herself composed plays and dictated them to her
governess. Why dictate them? Because nobody had gotten around to
giving her writing lessons. Finally, at age eleven, she decided to write
to her father who was out of town, so she somehow managed to learn
how to pen a legible message to him.

In the provinces especially, such a haphazard education surprised
no one, but in the Capital, the usual home upbringing of Madame
de Genlis' time was more systematic than hers, if not more effective.
Then, in the last three decades of the century, competent governesses
came to be in far better supply both in and out of Paris. Families that
could afford it even imported them from England, Switzerland and
other fashionable foreign lands.

Home-educated girls enjoyed far more freedom than their con-
vent-bred contemporaries. They grew up with a good deal less of the
hothouse naïveté and prudishness that colored the convent atmosphere. Parents sometimes permitted them to go along to the theatre
with them. Although they could not attend the stylish convent balls,
there were plenty of dances for them in neighbor's homes or in their

Madame de Genlis Giving a Harp Lesson

own homes, dances held in the late afternoon and early evening before the more glamorous grownup balls. Mothers chaperoned their daughters who rarely left their side except to dance. Still, they did dance, and they even went on occasion to public dance halls to watch the married ladies do the minuet, the *allemande* and, late in the century, the scandalously intimate waltz.

The home-bred young ladies had more frequent and closer contact with men, and it was not unusual for a male friend of the family to lace up a teenage girl or harass her with bristly kisses and bear hugs. Contact and familiarity with the opposite sex made these girls more capable of formulating their own opinions about men than their convent cousins. And they usually had a bigger say in the choice of a mate.

Critics of the home education and partisans of the convent found the free and easy atmosphere of certain fashionable residences far more dangerous than the refined, unworldly sanctity of a *monastère*. But in the second half of the eighteenth century, home rearing won the battle. More and more families followed the new trend. Flighty women of high society adapted with amazing rapidity to the new dewy-eyed image of the Good Mother Who Guides Her Daughter, and the patient, maternal, simple but sublime matron of Chardin's paintings found her imitators in the highest ranks of French society. We have only to remember Madame Vigée-Lebrun's portraits of Queen Marie-Antoinette herself, surrounded by her children, and the profoundly touching letter that this misguided woman wrote to them on the eve of her execution. Parents and children were growing closer in the domestic environment. Even noble families began to reject the solution of a convent education for their daughters, and by the end of the century, most young girls, noble or middle class, went to convents for one year only, to prepare for their first communion.

In the lowest classes of France, parents did not lose sleep pondering whether they should educate their girls in a convent or at home. For most of them, their daughter's minds were the least of their problems. And even if they could have afforded to send their girls to dorm at the Pentemont or the Ursulines, the good nuns would have pulled the welcome mat in as fast as you could say "Ecrasez l'Infâme." Boarding convents for lower-class girls did not exist. Throughout the provinces village priests provided primary instruction for them. And in Paris, for centuries chanters of various parishes had directed primary schools called *petites écoles,* some for boys, others coeducational and still others strictly for girls. These were free to children of the proletariat, but the petite bourgeoisie paid a small fee. A number of priests opened other primary schools called *écoles de charité* which were entirely free, and certain of these accepted girls. Throughout the eighteenth century the Paris convents instituted charity day programs, similar to trade schools, in which girls from poor families could learn sewing, embroidery or other practical skills free of charge.[20]

Obviously, a real effort was being made to bring instruction to young males and females of the lower classes. In 1724, a government decree stipulated that every parish in France should have teachers for boys and girls and that all parents should send their children to school. Unfortunately, this promising attempt at compulsory education failed, for the law was not put into practice. It would have been too much to expect: although many communities were trying their utmost to combat ignorance and illiteracy in lower-class males and females, there was no universal or standard policy that could serve as a guide for educators. When it came to the female poor specifically, the situation seemed hopeless. Competent instructresses were scarce and money for female education even scarcer. Government subsidies were out of the question, and local councils could not imagine allocating funds for such a cause. What? Establish a free school for girls in our village? But that would be taking food out of the mouths of the poor. There is simply not enough money. If we consented to such a proposal, the price of food and other necessities would jump sky high. Female instruction? Just a pretext, a hoax![21] Finally, many parents themselves, especially provincial ones, mistrusted teachers, male or female, and balked at the idea of giving their daughters a fancy, newfangled school education.

So progress was slow, and the rudimentary instruction provided for girls of the common people poked along in fits and starts. It really did not make any remarkable headway until the second half of the nineteenth century, when organized educational policies finally gave it impetus and direction.

Mediocre grades go then to the mediocre eighteenth-century education for women. We cannot even say indulgently, "It was a good education for its time," since precisely within its time so many people condemned it as frivolous and inadequate. As in previous years, girls were taught less than boys. The example of Voltaire's school, the Lycée Louis-le-Grand, may seem an unfair one, since the Jesuit fathers there instructed the fair-haired sons of the cream of Paris nobility and haute bourgeoisie. But in what upper-class convent or home could a girl find anything approaching the classic foundation and the encouragement to creativity that budding male intellectuals received from Fathers Porée and Tournemine? The sad truth was that at any social level, a woman's education did not compare with a man's.

Then whence came Madame du Châtelet and her treatises on happiness or her studies on Newton? What of Madame de Genlis and her interminable list of publications? And all the brilliant salon directresses of the eighteenth century? They were, like other clever ladies of that period, largely self taught. At precisely the age when twentieth-century girls prepare to go off to college, they were preparing to wed. It was after marriage that they filled the lacunae quietly neglected by convent and home instruction, that they read, listened, discussed, wrote and impressed philosophers and artists with their sensitivity, understanding and knowledge.

So the question of convent or home was an academic one. Although in the final analysis the home was judged to be the healthier atmosphere of the two, neither one was terribly satisfactory, since, as we have seen, each had its academic and social pitfalls. What really counted was what a woman did with her life beyond her "formal" education. Ultimately, it was up to the individual female to chart her own intellectual course.

If the eighteenth-century education of Frenchwomen was, on the whole, uninspired and unimpressive, a few rosy spots make the picture less gloomy. The second half of the century, in particular the last two or three decades, did show promise. After 1750, the sciences began to interest an increasingly enlightened public. And this public included many women. What such women couldn't understand from their reading they could absorb in private lessons. But so much could be understood from reading those days, given the conversational, flirtatious style of a *philosophe* like Fontenelle, or the lucid and witty dialogues of a Voltaire. Besides, from 1757 on,[22] women and even

young girls could quite easily attend the new public courses given by
well-known scholars in Paris and throughout the remote provinces.[21]
Guided visits to botanical gardens, field trips to natural science
museums or nature walks in the mountain, an afternoon watching
eighteenth-century astronauts take off in a balloon from the Champ
de Mars—activities like these began to replace the languorous stroll
around the Tuileries or the extra cup of tea with Madame de This-or-
That.

The writer Thomas was not impressed. He claimed that back in
the sixteenth century, ladies did their learning out of sheer enthusiasm for knowledge itself, while eighteenth-century female intellectuals studied out of coquettishness; their knowledge, like their
jewelry, was more convincing as display than as genuine wealth. But
let us quickly bypass this murky question of sincerity and take stock
of a few hopeful signs.

A *Ladies' Journal (Journal des dames)* saw the light in 1759; its
aim was to keep women informed about noteworthy trends in literature and science. From 1764 on, its publishers were women. A little
later, in the last twenty years of the century, Frenchwomen had
access to a whole series of long, multi-volume texts called "libraries,"
devised to instruct women on any important subject that they wished
to master: history, astronomy, mathematics, etc. These *bibliothèques
des dames* were enormously successful, although they, like other
publications for females, reached almost exclusively the women of
the upper classes for whom they were written.

More significant for the future of women's education: the prerevolutionary and revolutionary periods spawned a number of "programs," "projects" and "plans" to improve the existing (or
non-existent) educational system for females. Many of these encouraged the separation of church and school. Madame de Miremont and Riballier hinted at the possibility of lay education for girls.
President Rolland of the Paris Parlement proposed this openly in
1772 and 1783. Condorcet, in his Report and Proposal for a Decree
on the General Organization of Public Instruction, went so far as to
suggest subsidizing lay schools by confiscating outright the revenues
of all existing convents.[23] If Condorcet's sense of justice seems to have
strayed egregiously on this point, when it came to education, his goal
was equality: equality of educational opportunity for all classes and
for both sexes.

A Dramatic Reading in Madame Geoffrin's Salon (David)

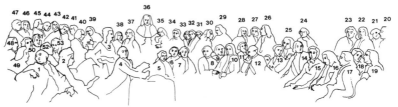

1, Buffon. 2, Mlle Lespinasse. 3, Mlle Clairon. 4, Le Kain. 5, D'Alembert. 6, Carl Vanloo. 7, Helvétius. 8, Duclos. 9, Piron. 10, Crébillon. 11, Bernis.

12, Duc de Nivernais. 13, Duchesse d' Anville. 14, Le Prince de Conti. 15, Mme Geoffrin. 16, Fontenelle. 17, Joseph Vernet. 18, Comtesse d'Houdetot. 19, Montesquieu. 20, Clairault. 21, D'Aguesseau. 22, Mairan. 23, Maupertuis. 24, Maréchal de Richelieu. 25, Malesherbes. 26, Turgot. 27, Diderot. 28, Quesnay. 29, Barthélemy. 30, Caylus. 31, Danville. 32, Soufflot. 33, Bouchardon. 34, St Lambert. 35, D'Argental. 36, Bust of Voltaire. 37, Duc de Choiseul. 38, Hénault. 39, Rameau. 40, Rousseau. 41, Raynal. 42, La Condamine. 43, Thomas. 44, Vien. 45, Marmontel. 46, Marivaux. 47, Gresset. 48, Bernard de Jussieu. 49, Daubenton. 50, Abbé de Condillac. 51, Madame de Graffigny. 52, Réaumur. 53, Madame du Bocage. (5)

The Revolution itself did nothing to promote all the ambitious plans proposed for equality in women's education. As a matter of fact, it broomed them swiftly into the back closet and banged the door shut. But at least now such ideas had been conceived—the eighteenth century had finally, with its last gasp, given them birth; they could now lie dormant until the nineteenth century was ready to discover and nurture them.

These were the good signs. On the eve of the Revolution, the foundation for sexual equality in education had been laid, and the actual level of feminine education in France had risen perceptibly above what it had been in the first years of the century. The quantity and quality of education that women received still could not compare to the brand of instruction available to men. But an upperclass woman could bridge the gap—by making herself man's intellectual equal and, at times, even his superior. The career of that wealthy bourgeoise, Madame Geoffrin, illustrates this dramatically. Her salon attracted the most outstanding *philosophes* of her time and she could converse, if not brilliantly, at least respectably, with all of them. One day, an habitué of the Geoffrin dinners, noticing that another customary guest was absent, asked his hostess, "Where is that quiet gentleman—the man who always sat at the end of the table at dinner and never said a word? Madame Geoffrin replied, "That, sir, was my husband: he died last week."[24]

*   *   *   *   *

We have now arrived at some partial answers to the question of sexual equality in the eighteenth century. For a broader understanding of this question, let us reach for another yardstick, one that will apprise us of the official rights or duties of the eighteenth-century Frenchwoman—the yardstick of the Law.

4

The Scales of Justice

Stitch by stitch or stone by stone, a legal structure had slowly arisen to form an arch around women. Was it a fortress or a prison? An armor or a straightjacket? The code of laws that men devised in order to "protect" their weaker mammals was indeed a strange sanctuary, for it legitimized the concept of woman's inferiority and established once and for all her subservience to man. This was the legal inheritance of the eighteenth-century Frenchwoman.

The legacy had been passed down by fifth-century German invaders of Gaul, by the Catholic church and by ancient Roman lawmakers—and to this day historians are not sure which of the three to blame. Perhaps the German barbarians had set the pattern with their quasi-military family structure dominated by the omnipotent *Meister.* But later the civilizing Roman law, in some ways more lenient than this Germanic tradition, did little to change the male-supremacy picture. It merely provided custom with a handy set of written rules.

The Church appears to have introduced a hopeful note, by stressing the unity of the married couple, fused into one fleshly being through love. Woman, whose image might have been shaped for eternity by that primordial villainess, Eve, now had a more flattering fate in the aureole of the Virgin Mary. And if modern females feel numb on a pedestal and shackled in a halo, medieval French ladies were positively delighted with their new sanctity. Noblewomen like Aliénor d'Aquitaine and her daughter Marie de Champagne encouraged their southern troubadours toward a poetry of enthralled male submissiveness. The Age of Chivalry was short-lived, however, and its principles were restricted to a relatively narrow segment of courtly society. Woman's fate had not altered preceptibly, for the Church, following Hebraic law, still considered females inferior creatures and continued to insure their subservience to male protectors.

For centuries, the laws that applied to the women of France varied from province to province, since no national legal system existed to coordinate them. Northern and parts of central France followed local Celtic or Germanic customs. Farther south, certain provinces had taken and adapted to their needs ancient codified Roman law. Even as late as the eighteenth century, legal standards that governed females continued to differ preceptibly in various regions of France.[1] Yet, whether northern or southern, customary or codified, whether based on Roman, barbaric or canon regulations, whether enforced to the letter by a rigorous judge or circumvented by a more indulgent soul, all of these laws spelled out the very same message, woman's inferiority, and all emphasized milady's Duty while utterly ignoring such little-known Rights as feminine liberty and equality.

Strangely enough, the eighteenth-century Frenchwoman was in some ways even worse off than her maternal ancestors of the Dark Ages. In those remote days a daughter did not need her father's consent to marry. A girl of twelve and a boy of fourteen could, according to Church law, wed of their own accord. In an era when so many men were busy warring for religion, power or sheer survival, women were quite active on the local political stages. They voted in town meetings, for example, went as deputies to the States General and for some time they were even peers in *parlements.* Abbesses founded convents, gave out directives, participated in regional political assemblies through the intermediary of private lawyers. Wives and widows of noblemen acted as *seigneurs,* administering property, taking in taxes, hearing complaints and settling disputes. And until the fourteenth century, queens truly ruled as queens. Philippe V changed that practice when he found it unsuitable to his power politics, and from his time on a French king's wife was legally queen in name only: she no longer wore a sovereign's crown.

If this contrast between the legal status of eighteenth-century and medieval women cannot exactly be called "paradise lost," it is clear that at least some forms of feminine power had disappeared. To add insult to injury, from the seventeenth century on, any time that woman was officially relegated to the shadows, somebody invoked the ghost of *propter imbecillitatem sexus,* and, alas, the Latin phrase suggested not only weakness but mental incapacity of females. This was clearly not progress. At least in barbarian times, a woman could be assured that she was worth as much as a man, for if she was killed her murderer paid exactly the same amount of retribution as if the victim had been a man (even more if the victim was pregnant).

But let us leave the days of militant Brunhildes, days when bridegrooms provided dowries and when a Genevieve or a Joan could win sainthood by saving Paris or all of France from the hands of the enemy. The time is the eighteenth century, and a Frenchwoman now had to reckon with certain unsavory legal realities. The most glaring of these was her status as a married woman.

Her husband was officially Lord and Master. Lest there be the slightest doubt about that, the law spelled it out in no uncertain terms: "Marriage, which forms a society, that of husband and wife dominated by the husband, gives said husband, in his capacity of chief of this society, the right of power over his wife's person."[2] On marrying, the bride moved into lodgings inhabited or chosen by the groom or his family, and from then on she was bound to follow her husband wherever he wished. If this fate did not appeal to her, so much the worse. She could only escape it if he had committed some crime or had gone totally berserk. The new bride took not only the name but the rank of her husband. As enchanting as this may have been for the bourgeoise who said "I do" to a title, it hardly suited the aristocratic lady who had to sacrifice her nobility when she married. Moreover, males, not females, passed nobility on to their heirs.

Now so far these examples of a husband's "power over his wife's person" can scarcely move us to tears or stir us to ardent protest. A more serious cause for complaint would be his legal "power of correction." According to Germanic law, any self-respecting husband could beat up his wife once in a while. Then, from the Renaissance on, physical abuse could, at times, give an indignant lady grounds for separation. But most often this depended on the frequency and ferocity of the beating and on whether the little woman's health was really endangered by it. An article in the eighteenth-century *Encyclopédie* informs us with a certain optimism that "In present-day France, a husband can really not chastise his wife with impunity."[3] But the qualifier "with impunity" could allow for a good bit of leeway. And ultimately this matter of wife beating came down to class. The legal expert of the day, Robert Pothier, tells us that a husband's slap or punch "can be cause for separation among well-bred couples, but not among lower-class people, unless [the violence] is repeated frequently."[4]

The eighteenth-century Frenchman's power over his wife's person extended to her earthly goods as well. Witness the dowry. A husband acted as trustee of his wife's marriage portion; he could not dispose of it but neither could she do so without his consent. This capital was a sort of insurance: if the couple separated or if the husband died before his wife, her dowry returned to her, and if his death followed hers the children inherited it. Still, during his lifetime, a married man had rights to any revenue accruing from his wife's dowry, for this was intended to help him cover various expenses incurred by his marriage.[5] In the north of France, the property arrangements of married couples centered not on the dowry but on the *community* system. Community property referred to the money and other possessions that a husband and wife would pool at the time of their marriage. Theoretically the wife held one-half interest in this property for, unless she jeopardized her portion by living apart from her mate or committing adultery, she would get her share back if he died or if they separated.[6] But in point of fact, a woman's right to community property was only an eventual one, for while she lived with him, her husband exercised absolute power over it, even that part of it which she had contributed.

Marriage contracts often distinguished between community property and the wife's *personal effects*. These personal effects consisted on the one hand of "movable" property, that is stocks and bonds, legacies, regular income or objects of value, all administered by her husband; and on the other hand "immovable" possessions such as tracts of land or houses, over which she retained complete ownership but which she could lose through a husband's negligence (for example, in case he did not pay taxes due on them). Whatever wifely money or goods were not positively stipulated as "personal effects" in the marriage contract became absorbed in the community property.[7] Only very exceptionally a separate-property clause in the contract spelled out a wife's continuing power over all of her own wealth during her marriage. Most often the community-property system prevailed with the husband enjoying full legal rights over part or all of his wife's possessions.

Now occasionally, amidst all this draconian legal apparatus, we find some favorable signs: clauses aimed not at the protection or control of a wife *by* her husband, but at her protection *from* him. This was the case with a wife's land or her dowry, for generally a husband could not fully appropriate them. We may wonder how such exceptions became law. Did some enlightened champion of women's rights urge this legislation? Not at all. If a husband had no legal right to take ownership of his wife's estate, it was not because of a humanitarian regard for the weaker sex. Essentially, these laws provided not for wives but for their kith and kin, for most families felt strongly that land had to remain in the blood line and revert to it if the husband died or became incompetent to administer it.

And even this safeguarding of a wife's estate worked curiously against her. The feudal system had established land as the major source of wealth and power in France. Yet, in the eighteenth century money, not land, was on the rise. The landed aristocracy, for all their prejudice against commerce, would soon bow down—or under—to bourgeois capitalism. However, a wife's income, her legacies, her stocks and bonds, could all be invested or alienated by a reckless husband, leaving her in sad financial straights indeed!

Wherever money was an issue, the eighteenth-century French wife ran headlong into a formidable barrage of "cannots." Without her husband's authorization she could not give away money or receive money due her, she could not pay creditors, enter into contracts, accept or refuse an inheritance. If by chance she did any of these things without his permission, he could demand nullification of her act. Even if the husband was a minor and his wife of age, she still needed his consent in such affairs. When it came to females making out wills, some provinces were more relaxed than others, reasoning, logically, that when a wife's will came into effect, she was no longer under her husband's jurisdiction. But in many provinces a dying woman was not allowed to draw up her last will and testament without her husband's consent.

Without permission from her spouse a woman could not engage in litigation either as a plaintiff or as a defendant. She could not serve as a witness for wills or other notarized acts,[8] although she could testify in court on civil or criminal matters. In past centuries some misogynistic observers of the legal scene claimed that three female witnesses equalled two (or fewer) male ones. The *Encyclopédie* informs us that this arithmetic was actually nowhere to be found in the law; the concept had simply developed from the understanding that women's testimony is usually more frivolous and contradictory than men's. Jaucourt, the author of this section of the article on women, concluded rather vaguely that "It depends on the judge's prudence to give more or less credence to women's testimony, according to the kind of woman who happens to be testifying, and other circumstances. . ."[9]

Certainly the eighteenth-century French wife's legal image appears as a bizarre distortion when viewed through twentieth-century lenses. She paid taxes but could not be a tax collector. She functioned as administrator of her household, did or supervised the shopping, but unless she was a business woman, she could not be held legally responsible for her debts or for any contract she might enter into—in some cases not even a contract with her own husband. But we find an even stranger contradiction, a contradiction that must have embarrassed any legal mind that fell on it. Any bachelor girl who was of age could buy, sell, give away money or possessions,[10] go to court, bring suit: legally she was very much her own person. But on the day of her marriage she sold all of these rights for a ring and a man who so often would come to mean very little to her.

How was this possible? Did a girl suddenly lose her competency with her virginity? Was there something in the married state that turned her from a capable human being into a blithering idiot, so irresponsible that she could not be held accountable for debts and contracts? The notion of the irresponsible, nonresponsible married female—a throwback to the Roman Senator-Consul Velleius who maintained that women had to be protected against their own weakness—had found its way into the French legal picture around the sixteenth century. The French government worked for many years to abolish the concept and to hold women liable for their debts and civil obligations. During the eighteenth century, the Velleian law of female nonresponsibility disappeared from the books. But the notion of female incapacity persisted like the fumes of cooked cabbage.

No observers of the legal scene managed to come up with a convincing explanation of the curious case of the competent single girl in sudden need of a husband's protection and authority. One common answer was family unity: a wife and mother had to be kept out of public affairs, business dealings and other independent action so that her family would remain united under the single authority of the male head-of-household. Many men and women felt that a wife had all she could handle (and all she should handle) just running the household and caring for her children. A less flattering explanation of the situation was that society itself needed protection from the chaos that might occur if married women were given a free rein in society.[11] But the legal mastermind Pothier denied that the rules governing wives had anything at all to do with feminine incapacity. At the heart of the whole matter lay the simple fact that in the eighteenth-century husband-wife community the male was still officially recognized by the law as chief-invested-with-full-power. French legal authority, said Pothier quite categorically, favored the husband and not the wife.[12] Here again was the cold juridical reality of the Roman, Germanic and even Christian concept of the husband as master.

In the hard light of these facts, it should come as no surprise that laws dealing with adultery were unfavorable to women. The Church bade husband and wife both "Love and be faithful to one another," but the law court championed the double standard. According to law, a wife had to presume that her husband was not cheating, for the plain and simple reason that "It is not up to the wife, who is an inferior, to question the conduct of her husband, who is her superior."[13] The conduct of a wife, however, was another thing entirely.

Back in the sixteenth century an adulterous woman discovered in flagrant delight could expect a rather picturesque punishment. After a sound beating with switches (sometimes after three of them) she might be led through the streets of her town wearing two hats, each a different color, and her dress pulled far up to expose her undergarment to the eyes of a jeering crowd. But by the eighteenth century, Madame had come a long way. A more dignified punishment now replaced this sort of brutal farce. After a solemn family meeting or two, her husband could, on procuring a "lettre de cachet," have his erring wife put away in a convent for two years. If he was still interested in her, he could visit her there and could take her back when the two years of confinement were up. But if he decided not to welcome her home, as Pothier told it, "She must have her head shaved and stay in said convent the rest of her days; moreover, she is declared deprived of her dowry, jointure and any matrimonial contractual agreements.[14] Pothier added optimistically that if her husband died before she did, she could leave her convent quarters and even petition to remarry, that is, if she got any offers at that stage of the game.

Was this incarceration of adulteresses actually practiced at that time? The Goncourt brothers insist that outside of novels women were rarely pushed into convents against their will, and yet we find examples enough of unfaithful eighteenth-century women who suffered such a fate. The archives of Police Chief D'Argenson reveal that early in the century the high-ranking Duchesse de Mazarin (Marquise de Richelieu) unwillingly entered the Couvent des Filles Anglaises, that the Chanoinesse de Bretteville went just as reluctantly to the Ursulines de Châteaubriant and Madame de Montmorency, niece of the Bishop of Montauban, to the Benedictine convent at Issoire. The first two ladies managed to escape; the third pleaded for liberty and won it somehow. The Goncourts themselves tell us how, later in the century, imprudent wives of noblemen were thrown into cabs and, accompanied by armed guards, carted away to correctional convents like the Bon-Pasteur:

> Often they were even carried off from a brilliant supper, brutally snatched away from enjoyment, like that Madame de Sainville, so wildly in love with Clairval: they seized her dressed in all her finery right in the midst of preparations for the Duchesse de Mirepoix's ball. They took her from her women, locked her personal maid up in Sainte-Pélagie,[15] and took her to the Filles de Sainte-Marie in Nancy, where she didn't have a cent to her name. In just the same way they carted off President Portail's wife and Madame de Vaubecourt and Madame d'Ormesson. And in the same way they put away. . . Madame d'Hunolstein who, cloistered and converted, became such an exemplary penitent.[16]

The enforced convent sequestration was, indeed, frequently a subject for novels. But in general, eighteenth-century prose literature all too accurately reflected the society of its time. This vengeful practice did abate toward the end of the century when a new tolerance frowned on such archaic procedures. The rule, however, remained on the books.

A betrayed wife, on the other hand, had little recourse. Divorce was unheard of and legal separations were difficult to obtain, especially in the first half of the century. A woman could procure a separation only if her husband's violent treatment threatened her health or life, if he defamed her in public or had her sequestered through false accusations. She could not leave a husband who was merely unfaithful or one who had gone out of his mind. The case of a husband with a raging venereal disease left room for debate; the individual judge had to grapple with that one according to his own conscience.[17] In the last part of the century it became much easier to procure a legal separation. As a matter of fact, the writer Mercier exclaimed that separating had become the latest fashion in Paris.

The sexual inequality that dominated marriage laws held sway just as forcefully over matters of inheritance. In many regions of France girls with brothers had no right to their deceased parents' fortune. The eldest son received almost everything, while his sisters could only hope for a dowry substantial enough to buy into a good marriage. The idea of masculine inheritance was certainly not a feature of the old Roman law, for the Romans divided their legacy equally among their sons and daughters. The practice was relatively modern for all its trite inequity. From the fifteenth century on, Paris adopted the Roman rule of inheritance without sexual discrimination—but only in *non-noble* families. After all, an important patrimony had to be perpetuated through the ages, and this could only be assured if the males of an aristocratic family did the inheriting. In provinces like Auvergne, Béarn and Normandie, masculine inheritance was the rule in the eighteenth century. When an unmarried girl survived her parents, her brothers became her guardians.[18]

Up to this point the picture of the eighteenth-century Frenchwoman's legal situation has added up to a catalog of duties and restrictions with hardly a trace of rights: a monotonous litany of don'ts, no's and cannot's. It is somewhat refreshing then to find that a

French mother had a few modest privileges: she could hold as a widow the rights of legal guardianship of her children and tutelage of their possessions. If the situation warranted, she could exercise the same rights over her grandchildren too. And in certain regions of customary law a woman could be guardian of her brothers, sisters and even of her husband if he happened to be raving mad. But she could not act as guardian or legal tutor of anyone outside of her immediate family, "because of the weakness of her sex."[19]

In case anyone wondered how such an incompetent was able to take legal charge of her family, the explanation was that "it is presumed that [her] maternal tenderness can compensate for what [she] otherwise lacks."[!][20] Even a mother's guardianship of her own children carried some restrictions. For example, as a widow, she could lose this privilege if she remarried or if her relatives disapproved of her choice of a husband for her young charge. When it came to marrying off children in general, a mother usually had far less say than her husband. A father had no need to justify his choice of a son-in-law, but his wife was obliged to justify hers. If she persisted in arranging a marriage that the rest of her family disapproved of, she could be legally forced to make an aboutface. Until 1729, in some sections of France, mothers could inherit nothing from their deceased children.

Within the framework of a patently antifeminist legal system, it made extraordinary sense to be a widow, more precisely, the widow of a rich husband. Such a woman enjoyed relative freedom and the use of her late husband's fortune. She could enter into contracts or litigation and could do what she would with her possessions. But, as usual, there were strings: if she wished to remarry, as generous as she might feel, she could not simply hand her late husband's wealth over to her new groom—her former in-laws could prevent such a move. Nor could she marry a man socially inferior to herself (although a widower was free to wed his housemaid if he liked). Moreover, if a widow wasn't careful about going through a respectable period of mourning, she could be taken to court and could theoretically be deprived of her dower. Needless to say, there were no such legal and moral restrictions placed on widowers.

Fortunately, toward the end of the century, certain laws discriminating against women were abolished. An ancient edict permitting a man to thrash his wife so long as he didn't quite kill her fell happily into disuse. Another one, dating from the sixteenth-century reign of Henri II, obliged any unwed pregnant girl to declare her condition to government officials, although she was not forced to name the father of her child. If the infant died before being baptized, the girl could be held to the death penalty. This punishment had come about as an official attempt to decrease the large number of infanticides plaguing the French nation, but such an understandable goal inspired dubious methods indeed. Customary law even provided for a frequent physical verification of pregnancy. If parents suspected that their unmarried daughter's fainting fits were not from tight undergarments, they could invite a midwife to visit her. If their worst fears were justified, the midwife would keep in touch with the girl to make sure that nothing interfered with her pregnancy. In the eighteenth century unwed mothers were somewhat better off.[21] The threat of the death penalty that hung over a girl whose child died before baptism was commuted to the threat of branding and banishment. And although as late as 1776, some girls still suffered the indignities of the verifying midwife's visit, the Parlements of Paris, Dijon and other cities had already abrogated this law.

As for "proper" young girls, they enjoyed certain new advantages in the last part of the century, for instead of the rigidly arranged marriage that had been the accepted rule in French society, wedding parleys now commonly included young daughter's opinion on whom she should have as her life's companion. This became true even in old noble families that had been quite accustomed to cut and dried commercial marriage "deals."

Also on the brighter side, Léon Abensour notes that in all provinces throughout France some women continued to exercise certain feudal rights that females had held since the Middle Ages. In the center and south of France especially, and in Brittany, female *seigneurs* owned and administered property and were legally responsible for themselves and their possessions.[22] These noble lady "lords" could give and receive homage, collect certain kinds of taxes, invest judges, name police sergeants, notaries, even jailors of royal prisons, and they needed no male authorization to do so. In Brittany, the Marquise de Mirabeau, in Lorraine, Anne Palatine de Bavière, along with abbesses of important French abbeys and other noblewomen, enjoyed privileges and power that contrasted sharply with the legal condition of most women of France. These female *seigneurs* could participate at meetings of local political bodies known as provincial "Estates" *(états provinciaux)*, in which they could theoretically hold seats. In fact, in the seventeenth century Madame de Sévigné did sit in the Brittany Estates. Then, during the eighteenth century, this practice became rare. Yet these noblewomen with fiefs, like nuns, female heads of families and leading members of feminine corporations were, until just before the Revolution, entitled to take part in elections of the Estates, and some of them actually did so. Until 1789, for example, the abbesses of Remiremont acted as judges in the district around their abbey and voted for the deputies of the Lorraine Estates.

Then the Revolution swept through France, brooming out these age-old rights of women along with any other reminders of feudal privileges.

*   *   *   *   *

The legal condition of the eighteenth-century Frenchwoman can only appear bleak, repressive and untenable from a modern woman's vantage point. Excluded from public office and many professions, "sheltered" from civic affairs, barred from principal inheritance rights, denied the freedom to administer her own possessions, placed often at the mercy of her husband but forbidden divorce, she could be well assured that in the dim rays of the law, sexual equality was nowhere in sight. Most radically affected by this was the noblewoman who had to be made and maintained the legal inferior of her spouse for the sake of her husband's aristocratic lineage. Luckier from the legal standpoint was the common woman who ran a shop or a business of her own. She, at least, had her own "civil personality," and she was responsible for her worldly possessions.

As we have seen, in the course of the French Enlightenment, a few harshly discriminatory laws were abrogated and some others were simply not put into practice any longer, but the bulk of these sexual inequities remained officially valid. There was no question of any judicial liberalization or any significant reform of laws concerning women during the eighteenth century.

Surely this situation would have been enough to prompt women to riots if they had thought about it. But the fact is that before the Revolution hardly any of them thought about it very much. One reason for this apparent apathy is that, in spite of the stirring protest of Beaumarchais' Marceline,[23] and in spite of all the unfair legislation that we have described here, the eighteenth-century Frenchwoman was not a poor victim at the mercy of this archaic set of regulations. For actually, a world of difference lay between the lawbooks and the lawcourts, between the stifling letter and the flexible spirit of the law. What with the wide variations among laws of different provinces, the large number of contradictions and obscurities found in legal texts and the perpetual changes and modifications wrought by King and *parlements,* it was up to the individual judges to do the interpreting as they thought best, and these judges had great leeway.[24] More often than not their interpretations of laws affecting women were quite liberal. They were indeed so liberal at times that an activist who was always quick to point out social injustices and who acerbically attacked the frivolous education foisted on young women, the writer Sébastien Mercier, saw the law courts as discriminating against the oppressed French husband. Bad enough, thought Mercier, that the Paris laws were making Parisian ladies so imperious and demanding, but that was not all. A widower could go bankrupt trying to restore his late wife's dowry to her family after paying her medical bills for years. And just see what happens when a married couple appear before a judge:

> A man and wife are on the outs? From the first the husband is in the wrong. She paints him in the most atrocious colors. Lawyers, laws and the verdict may be in his favor. But all of that is overturned in another court.[25]

If Mercier was exaggerating, at least he helped put the legal picture in perspective for us. And if we peruse the literary works of the French Enlightenment, works so full of social polemic, so broad in scope, so ambitious in liberal intent, we find that outside of Beaumarchais' *Figaro* they are singularly lacking in any descriptions of the legal victimization of females. On the contrary, the father-dominated seventeenth-century ingenue of Molière's plays has become the Marivaux heroine who must be sure of her fiancé before she consents to marry him. The vulnerable, pathologically blushing heroine of the old sentimental novel is now the self-assured eighteenth-century female character who is eternally engaged in some lawsuit, in apparent possession of her person and, sooner or later, of substantial material wealth. Beaumarchais himself presented an optimistic view of the feminine picture in the *Barbier de Séville* in which the nubile minor, Rosine, easily outmaneuvers her legal guardian, Bartolo, despite his insistence that "We are not in France, where women are always in the right!"[26]

In the final analysis, especially in the second half of the century, the Law seemed less a straitjacket than a pesky anachronism. It might have given an enlightened Frenchwoman food for thought. It obviously did not cramp her style.

Beaumarchais (Nattier)

5

The Reign of Women?

How satisfying it would be to close the lid and tie some spruce pink-ribbon conclusions over a satin-lined case containing the perfect likeness of an eighteenth-century Frenchwoman. How tempting it would be to survey the whole of history and proclaim categorically: "In spite of crushing legal restrictions and social pressures, eighteenth-century Frenchwomen were more powerful than ever before or ever again." Or, to conclude negatively (with fervor), "In spite of a superficial, overrated prestige, women of that time were more oppressed than ever." And yet the history of Frenchwomen up to the end of the Age of Enlightenment can be seen neither as a dramatic rise to power nor as a stunning fall from Grace. Throughout the centuries their role had shifted constantly. At one moment their strength lay in political prerogatives or involvement in literature and the arts and their weakness in a domestic servitude. In another area their situation seemed reversed, or at least quite different.

As for the eighteenth-century Frenchwoman, we cannot attempt to explain her lot unless we preface any answers with the words "It depends." For it depended, as we have seen, on her social and economic class, her age and marital status and on the angle from which we observed her: legal, pedagogical, political, moral and so on.

Once this has been said, we may view somewhat more lucidly both
the pluses and the minuses of her situation and the role she played.

The brilliance of the role that certain Frenchwomen did play at
the time owed much to the stages available to them. Just as the
renowned eighteenth-century actress Clairon would probably have
remained unknown and unsung in the early seventeenth century,
before Louis XIV had amalgamated the Paris theatres into the illustrious Comédie-Française, so a Madame de Tencin and a Duchesse
de Grammont would be mere shadows of their eighteenth-century
selves in our present democratized society. Several prestigious stages
were, indeed, open to women.

The most obvious sphere of influence was the Court, and women
of a certain class—even a lowborn Antoinette Poisson*—could share
in the machinations of court life. The world of finance was opening
up too, and the bourgeoisie got richer ever day: wives, daughters,
widows and paramours of the powerfully wealthy could all aspire to
a slice of the pie. And what of the possibilities in literature, philosophy, art and science? If we consider these fields with a cold eye, they
seem to have lost some of their luster in the 1700's. The theatre no
longer produced masterpieces worthy of Molière, Corneille and Racine. Eighteenth-century philosophy was purposely unsystematic,
and while refuting Descartes, it offered few original answers to replace his thought. French painting had its Watteau and its Fragon-
ard, but French music paled in comparison with the Italian product
and could only come up with Rameau for real competition. As for
science, Buffon popularized the exciting realm of natural history and
Lavoisier made his substantial contributions to chemistry and physics, but most of the important discoveries in physics, chemistry,
biology or astronomy were made prior to the Enlightenment or
afterwards. Yet the fields of literature, the arts and sciences captivat-
ed the imagination of eighteenth-century men and women and provoked great enthusiasm, especially among members of the French
bourgeoisie. This was, after all, the age of *lumières,* the age of
philosophers, of the *Encyclopédie* and of Voltaire. Cultured ladies of
the day were busy writing poetry, plays or pedagogical treatises, and
any woman with enough contacts and capital could summon fashionable writers and artists to dinner twice a week and thereby launch
her own "salon".

*Madame de Pompadour

So opportunities beckoned to women, who quickly answered the unwritten invitation to play a part in society. They took their places. At the top of the ladder reigned the uncrowned queens and mistresses. Too many books have been written about the fabulous Pompadour, the upstart DuBarry and the radiant Marie-Antoinette to warrant paragraphs about them here. Let us remember, however, that generals, cardinals and ministers were made or undone in the privacy of the royal boudoir and that milady's approval or disapproval could even mean the difference between war and peace. Witness the scoreboard drawn up by the Goncourt brothers:

> The Cardinal de Tencin obeys Madame de Tencin, Madame d'Estrades has the Comte d'Argenson in tow, the Duc de Choiseul is led around by the Duchesse de Grammont, without whom he might have accepted DuBarry's peace offerings, Madame de Langeac has the final word on the *Lettres de cachet* that Terray sends out, Mademoiselle Renard passes on army officers' promotions that Monsieur de Montbarrey has the king sign, Mademoiselle Guimard on the ecclesiastical benefices that Jarente hands out . . .[1]

And how many bright male stars owed their eclipse wholly or in part to the hostility of a woman in high court circles: the Comte d'Argenson vanquished by Pompadour, Choiseul by DuBarry, Turgot and Necker by Marie-Antoinette, and so on. The writer Marmontel, who listened carefully to Madame de Tencin's advice to take women for friends, found that the formula could succeed, indeed, even by accident. When Madame de Pompadour singled him out of her group of visitors, after five minutes alone with her, Marmontel returned to a roomful of broad smiles. Madame had simply given him back a manuscript that he had asked her to read and correct, but in a flash the author received enough dinner invitations to last him a week. A distinguished titled acquaintance approached him, took his hand and murmured earnestly, "So you don't speak to your old friends any more?"[2]

The feminine gender—singular or plural—was a most likely key to social and economic success. Dancourt knew it; Montesquieu knew it. Marivaux, well aware of the fact, wrote a novel, *The Parvenu Peasant (Le Paysan parvenu)*, in which the hero's social climb owes everything to his attractiveness to affluent bourgeoises of parliamentary and financial circles. As Jean-Jacques Rousseau put it:

[These women] have a natural ability to get what they ask for, even from their own husbands, not because they are their husbands but because they are men, and it is understood that no man will refuse a woman, not even his wife.[3]

In the world of letters and the arts the feminine touch was even more obvious. Not that women themselves achieved great success in these fields. In a period when France deemphasized literary style in favor of ideas and produced few literary masterpieces, no female writer could match a Madame de Lafayette or a Madame de Sévigné. As for the fine arts, Madame Vigée-Lebrun is the only eighteenth-century French woman painter remembered today.[4] The female contribution to cultural spheres was not one of creation but of influence, and this influence lay to a remarkable extent in the hands of salon directors like a Madame de Lambert or a Madame Geoffrin.

These women had become judges, arbiters of taste in drama and poetry and mediators in the realm of ideas and ideologies. Male writers—Montesquieu, Lesage, Rousseau and Mercier among them —constantly satirized or protested these trends, lamenting that such female directors of brain bureaus encouraged writers down the already wellworn path of frivolousness. If these protests did not provide proof enough that the salons and their directresses affected literature and ideas, we have only to look at some of Voltaire's and Diderot's dialogues which often strike us as refined and edited tape recordings of salon conversations.

Not only did salon directresses have an effect on the style and content of contemporary writings, they could also hold an author's fate in the palm of their hands. They acted as guardian angels, providing "their" writers with hospitality and protection that could sometimes mean the difference between a reputation and economic solvency or anonymity and starvation. Some observers felt that the angels of the salon did not actually discover and cultivate budding talent but only offered their protection once they had ample assurance that a writer was In. Madame Roland claimed that this was so with Madame Dupin who had shown herself lukewarm toward Jean-Jacques Rousseau until he made a name for himself. But be this true or not, Jean-Jacques' protectors and providers were inevitably well-known salon hostesses like Madame Dupin, Madame d'Epinay and Madame de Luxembourg.

The first step, perhaps the most important one for an aspiring writer, was to gain entrance into a salon, and any man of letters knew this well, for the final evidence was overwhelming. It was Madame de Lambert who presented Montesquieu to the Académie Française and Madame de Tencin who got Marivaux elected. Madame du Deffand did the same for D'Alembert, Madame Geoffrin for Marmontel (Madame de Tencin's advice paid off!), and after 1772, when D'Alembert became Perpetual Secretary of the Académie, his Julie de Lespinasse, who had left Madame du Deffand's employment to form her own salon, enjoyed tremendous recruiting powers. At least seven distinguished academicians could thank Julie for their immortality.

Through the doors of the salons passed diplomats, archeologists, painters, eminent foreign visitors like Walpole or Benjamin Franklin who did not miss the opportunity of being presented at the "Royal Court of the Rue Saint-Honoré," Madame Geoffrin's headquarters.[5] If, in the early decades of the century, conversation was gay and frivolous at the Duchesse du Maine's Court of Sceaux and literary in Madame de Lambert's salon, later it became more and more preoccupied with the new anti-religious ideas of the *philosophes.* In these elegant meeting places where a bourgeois intellectual could outshine a blue blood and where even a petit bourgeois painter could command respect, the tone grew increasingly liberal. The freethinking that Madame de Geoffrin kept discreetly under control became daring in the salon of a Julie de Lespinasse. And at the outbreak of the Revolution, when political preoccupations overshadowed philosophical ones, the tone could turn inflammatory in the home of a Madame Roland.

French women, although they were unaware of it, were now at a turning point.

In the course of the century a social and political thinker like Montesquieu could look around him and deplore the discrimination against Negroes or Jews. Yet, when it came to women, he might suggest certain laws that would affect their lives, such as one permitting divorce, for example—but he did not see them as a group that had been mistreated by society. Neither, as we have seen, did most other writers, for it would have been hard to imagine them oppressed while witnessing the dazzling spectacle of power that women exer-

cized on so many strategic fronts. As for the women themselves, they
were not yet conscious of themselves as a group or as a serious cause.
We found them still unactivated near the end of the century, just
before the outbreak of the Revolution, despite the increasingly agitat-
ed flow of pamphlets for and against their sex.

In 1789, when the Paris commonwomen began beating the drum
for their long trek to Versailles, they were thinking not of the feminist
cause but of the high price and scarcity of bread and of the aristocrats
whom they held responsible for their misery. Once the Revolution
had gotten under way, however, women stepped to the forefront and
began to play a highly active role, in salons (which were closed down
in 1792) or clubs, on the stage and in the street, although they were
not allowed to participate on revolutionary committees or to bear
arms.[6]

They did not all agree on everything. Some, like Olympe de
Gouges, wanted the Revolution but without the death of the King
and Queen; others, like Madame Roland, insisted that no one would
be free until the crowned heads were off. The Dutch self-styled
baroness revolutionary, Etta Palm Aelders, pushed for social and
moral reform. Others, not quite so high minded, were mainly intent
on dispatching aristocrats to the next world. Théroigne de Méricourt
and Pauline Léon were among the few to defend women's rights to
bear arms, and poor Olympe de Gouges vacillated with the consist-
ency of a ping pong ball between royalism and revolution. She vacillated most of all when it was her turn at the guillotine, pleading her
belly in vain: the powers that were opined that the unwed thirty-
eight-year-old Olympe wasn't pregnant enough. But in spite of differ-
ences and inconsistencies, a great number of women did agree on one
thing: action.

Now in times of revolution, action for some women has meant
militant and violent warfare. In the Revolution of 1848, Frenchwom-
en cut off the heads of military policemen; in 1871 their daughters,
known as *pétroleuses,* set fires in the capital. The long Revolution
of 1789 had more than its share of hard-line, even bloodthirsty
women: angry Jacobines who menaced and mistreated any females
who would not wear the tricolored cockade, armed "Amazons" who
militated in the high Pyrenees, terrorists like the Widow Barbier who
insisted that "things would not go right until all mean merchants,

former artistocrats and rich people are guillotined en masse."[7] Let us not forget those knitters at the guillotine, the *tricoteuses*. A modern researcher[8] tells us that the epithet "knitters" was not a derogatory one, for those ladies were busy making or collecting clothing and raising money for their revolutionary fighting men. Yet, as we think of these enterprising furies watching the heads roll in the Place de Grève, it is hard not to remember Dickens' Madame La Farge. And Suzanne Delaville's injunction to "purge the earth of monsters,"[8] in 1792, is almost worthy of our modern, terse "Off the pigs." It is striking to read the words of a tender wife and mother who was celebrated for her sentimental preromanticism—Madame Roland. In July, 1789, she warned friends:

> No, you are not free; nobody is yet. . . You're concerned about a municipality, and you're forgetting about heads that will conjure up new horrors. You are just children; your enthusiasm is merely straw fire, and if the National Assembly does not pass judgement on two illustrious heads [those of the King and Queen], you will all be screwed. . .[9]

This is the style adopted by many a revolutionary woman in the name of the Cause. If there were idealists among these women, Madame Roland was certainly one of them. Yet in so many of her contemporaries idealism was so solidly linked to brutality that we cannot believe the nineteenth-century historian Michelet when he tells glowingly, simplistically, how hundreds and thousands of Joans of Arc dragged a cannon and a lighted match to Versailles out of the kindness of their "noble hearts."[10] Still, whether out of hunger, frenzy, righteous indignation, egocentric theatrics, a love of excitement, an urge for power, generosity, anger, hatred, fellowship, fear, transcendent idealism or a million other reasons, to Versailles they went, and that abortive, unproductive, absurd gesture helped to launch women into the revolutionary foreground.

Soon women began to gather in clubs, joining men in their societies or forming all-female ones. The clubs encouraged philanthrophy, patriotism and virtue, in addition to a constant witch hunting and denunciation of enemies of the Revolution. Sisters, wives and mothers were now becoming polarized, not only to the revolutionary cause but—finally—to their own. With the progressive liberalization and ultimate disintegration of the French monarchy, with the tri-

Marie Antoinette and her Children (Vigée-Lebrun)

Marie Antoinette en Route to the Guillotine (David)

umph of the *philosophes* and their ideals of tolerance and freedom, the word "Duty" that had so colored the autocratic reign of Louis XIV, had finally been replaced by "Rights." That magic word was on everyone's lips. All manner of people registered complaints with the revolutionary administration; reports and official memoranda brought pleas for redress on the part of scores of formerly oppressed individuals or groups that were demanding their due. Now here were the women, fighting and contributing to the Revolution but kept neatly out of the decision-making process and relegated to their knitting and charity funds. Here they were barred from any public office and with no right to vote. Once the Revolution had raised their consciousness, other wounds began to fester. What about all the legal restrictions that made women second-class citizens? What about education? What about divorce?

In September, 1791, Olympe de Gouges jumped into the fray with a feminist manifesto patterned after Condorcet's "Rights of Man." She called it "Rights of Women and the Female Citizen." According to Olympe, the sex that was "superior in beauty as in courage, in maternal suffering,"[11] demanded universal suffrage, a right to public office, honors when merited and, in general, equality with men. At the same time the writer proposed a total revision of marriage in the form of a social contract which stressed the legal recognition of either partner's illegitimate children. The following year[12] Pauline Léon demanded women's right to arms and Etta Palm led a group of women to the Assembly where she argued logically that since women had shared in the dangers of the Revolution, why could they not share in the advantages? Etta Palm held that the government should admit females to civil and military posts, provide an education for girls and permit divorce.

There were some hopeful signs. In 1790 the revolutionary powers put an end to masculine inheritance; in 1792 they enacted a law permitting divorce (which, however, was revoked in the nineteenth century), and the Revolution did lay the foundation for improved education for girls. But at the time, most of women's demands were simply filed away or patently ignored. Olympe de Gouges protested in vain that women had the right to ascend the speaker's platform if they had the right to ascend the scaffold. For the men of the National Assembly, female support was all well and good but female demands were becoming tiresome and irritating. When Claire Lacombe (known by Lamartine and Michelet as "Rose") forced her way into the Chamber of the General Council in 1793, the Procuror, a Monsieur Charmette, is said to have cried out, "Since when are women permitted to renounce their sex and become men?"[13] Obviously, women could not be equal because they were *different.*

Here again was the old objection, the old fear that women would no longer be women. It came out most strongly in the final blow that the Revolution delivered to women and the budding feminist cause, when the Committee of Public Safety disbanded the highly active women's clubs in 1793. The committee reported that several "so-called Jacobines"[13] had been walking to market wearing men's pants and red bonnets, and in their revolutionary fervor they had tried to force other women they met to don the same costume. A fight ensued but was broken up by the authorities. That evening, same cause and same effect, but this time the fight resulted in a public disturbance. The upshot of the matter was that the Committee felt that women's organizations were becoming generally unreasonable in their demands and especially in their dogged insistence in taking an active part in government affairs. It was high time to put a stop to such nonsense. Most important, women had to remember that there was a *difference* between men and women and that the whole social order depended on this difference. In case the women could not grasp this fully, the Committee of Public Safety patiently spelled it out:

Man is strong, robust, born with a great energy, boldness and courage; he braves perils and the intemperance of seasons because of his physical constitution; he resists all the elements; he is competent in the arts and in difficult work; and since he, almost exclusively, is destined for agriculture, commerce, navigation, voyages, war and everything that demands force, intelligence, capability, likewise he alone is suited to the profound and serious meditation that demands great mental concentration and long study which women cannot manage.[14]

It is easy to guess that when the Committee of Public Safety painted Woman's portrait, it pictured her not behind a desk but squarely in the center of her household. Later, Napoleon would add the final touch by announcing, "If there is one thing that is not French it's a woman who does what she wants."[15]

Evidently, the only real equality that women achieved during the
Revolution was the one that Olympe de Gouges pointed out—the
right to be guillotined. Madame Roland, Lucille Desmoulins, the
anti-revolutionary Charlotte Corday, the King's wife and Olympe
herself were examples enough of this democracy in action. But
throughout the Revolution, women who actually demanded sexual
equality constituted only a small minority. Even those women who
fought long and hard for the republican cause remained vastly un-
concerned with the question. In fact they could almost echo the
woman's-place-is-in-the-home diatribes of the Committee of Public
Safety. Madame Roland had read Jean-Jacques, and although she
drafted many of her husband's speeches and even his famous letter
to Louis XVI, she was content to intrigue from behind the scenes and
to appear to be the incarnation of Rousseau's feminine ideal, a gentle,
modest Julie. Other well-known revolutionary wives like Lucille
Desmoulins devoted their energies not to feminism but, notably, to
providing moral support for their husbands.

The Revolution's contribution to feminism was that it polarized
a certain minority of women: it first made them politically active and
politically aware. In so doing it also made them aware of themselves
as a class and as potential citizens entitled to their rights. The Revolution, then, helped to crystallize the feminist cause and to postulate
it as a real cause. This budding campaign for sexual equality was
squashed at the end of the century and brushed into the imperial
closet—to emerge into daylight some decades later.

*   *   *   *   *

The gains that Frenchwomen made in the course of the eighteenth
century were perceptible although not very dramatic. Feminine education did not improve radically, but more and more people took the
subject seriously. As we have seen, certain discriminatory laws were
abrogated or ignored in the latter part of the century. And even
though marriages continued to be arranged by parents, nubile girls
did have a greater say in choosing their mates to be. But far more
striking than what these Frenchwomen acquired was what they
themselves became: how they evolved as women from one end of the
century to the other. Their metamorphosis was partly the cause and

partly the effect of the general metamorphosis in the intellectual and moral climate of the French Enlightenment, which ran its course from the frivolity and notorious debauchery of the Regency period, through the triumph of the *philosophes* and the glorification of science and into the preromantic sentimentality inspired by Rousseau.

In the early years, the paper doll of high society fretted and complained through her daily three-hour ritual of the *toilette,* then left her home painted and powdered to hear the same witticisms, the same gossip and the same slander at each of her visits, yawned through one boring play after another and mournfully lamented all the social duties that kept her on her merry-go-round—but of course she sacrificed none of them. Stylized nostalgia surrounded her: on chair coverings and Gobelin tapestries simple shepherds and shepherdesses gazed languorously at each other, oblivious of a suggestive madrigal that some fashionable *chevalier* was reciting to a bejewelled financier's wife. This idyllic Arcadia remained in the background, to take the spotlight only at the end of the era when Marie-Antoinette went "back to nature" in style, playing her elegant shepherdess role at Trianon.

Innocence, sentiment, simplicity and nature were well hidden but not dead. Certain traces of a sentimental reaction were in the air. In 1735, the libertine and wag Nivelle de la Chaussée, sensing that sentiment was becoming a very salable commodity, presented his *Stylish Prejudice (Le Préjugé à la mode)* at the Comédie Française. When the wordly nobleman Durval fell on his knees before his very wife in the last scene of the play, how many husbands in the audience must have fidgeted nervously under the righteously triumphant glances of their tear-drenched spouses. Soon other tearful dramas gave marital fidelity a good press, and all manner of didactic plays, inspired by heartrending English dramas, inundated the French stage. In the 1750's that master of wit, Denis Diderot, surpassed everyone with his embarrassing super-emotional *drames bourgeois.* The gay, self-sufficient Sylvias and Lisettes of the French Regency had become tender Constances and Sophies. Frenchwomen were now just about ready for Rousseau.

In an age when Eros was reduced to libido and Love to making love, imagine a woman who could inspire a holy passion in a man,

Old Woman (attributed to Chardin)

Madame Labille-Guiard and Two Students (self-portrait)

one to last him unfalteringly through his whole life. Such a woman
would have to be everything: feminine and alluring but not licentious, pensive but capable of gaiety, maternally wise but eternally
young and unpedantic. She would also love the simple things, exult
in nature, adore God and make a faithful, loving wife—in short, she
would be Julie, the heroine of Rousseau's *Nouvelle Héloïse,* and her
adoring lover would be his hero, Saint-Preux. Here was the image
that jaded Frenchwomen were unconsciously seeking. Rousseau captured and convinced them with his dream of innocence, of transcend-
ence, of salvation through love. They believed the dream and they
believed Rousseau when he drew them the portrait of the woman
who deserved such a destiny. They listened to this man who berated
them, who even insulted them, calling them superficial, mannish or
pretentious. Indeed, some even fell in love with that boor of a genius.
And many women who did not write him or try to see him to
convince him they were different, tried to convince themselves and
others of it.

The new soft, sweet and sentimental image did not suddenly con-
vert all women into Julies and Sophies. The aristocratic snuff hounds
of the first half of the century were followed as we have seen, by the
sword-bearing, pants-wearing furies of the Revolution. Later, Mercier complained that female timidity, simplicity and modesty had
disappeared, and he insisted, "They have gone too far to be able to
return to their sex. They will have to become men completely if they
don't want to lose ground."[16] And Restif de la Bretonne exclaimed:

> What! Am I to keep silent in a work like this when I see women blind
> to their true interests, imitating our style of dress, wearing low heels,
> while our fops keep wearing theirs higher, wearing hats, neglecting their
> figure, and when I see the press applauding this philosophical delirium,
> so dangerous for our morals? No! No! I shall tell women: To resemble
> men. . . is to profane your dress: it means that you are taking your sex
> from it, stifling nature's will, and you risk replacing [nature] with the
> frightful vice, which I don't dare name, [the vice] of the ancient Greeks
> and Romans.[17]

But Mercier and Restif need not have worried themselves. Although some women may have appeared shockingly virile at the
time, France was hardly ready for unisex. True, the dazzling hoop-

skirts did give way to simpler, slimmer post-revolutionary gowns, but the lines of the new fashion were soft and graceful, indicating that Frenchwomen had continued to substitute one feminine image for another. They had exchanged the paper doll for a more durable Julie model,[18] and the end of the century found them adapting effortlessly to the ideal of the virtuous Roman matron of David's republican paintings.

Morally and esthetically, in theory and in practice, the Frenchwoman kept her identity as one-half of the male-female dance team, her feminine steps following his masculine lead to the beat of another minuet. Women were still very much women, and yet something had changed in them besides the style of their dress, the pattern of their dance or the shape of their illusions. The women themselves had somehow changed. We find that those whom we meet in the latter part of the century project more authentically as individuals; with all their softness and gracefulness they are both interested and interesting people. Certainly, philosophers had written for and about women all through the French Enlightenment—but what a contrast between the pretty blonde Marquise who plays interlocutress in 1686 in Fontenelle's *Plurality of the Worlds* and Julie de Lespinasse who serves as intermediary in Diderot's *D'Alembert's Dream* in 1769. In the first case we meet a pouting, coquettish woman of the world who would be horrified if anyone thought of her as an intellectual; in the other a woman who grasps quickly and discusses the most challenging concepts fearlessly and soberly without affectation or flirtatious self-effacement.

The last decades of the century seemed to breathe self-assurance, warmth and life into Frenchwomen. Undoubtedly the trend toward a home education helped make this possible, for young girls became known to their parents, loved and understood as individuals rather than as commodities to be held in escrow, polished up and bartered off. But whatever the reasons for this change, women of the latter half-century come across more convincingly as human beings. A Geneviève de Malboissière, a Madame Roland or Julie de Lespinasse may have had their foibles and delusions, but how much more immediately their letters speak to us today than those of the scientifically philosophical Madame du Châtelet or the dry-witted Madame du Deffand.

What conclusions could today's feminists draw from this account of the eighteenth-century Frenchwoman? Undoubtedly negative or neutral ones, for we have discovered for one thing that her Reign was based on the famous difference: her femininity and her ability to exploit it to the fullest. For modern liberationists, that eighteenth-century brand of woman power would be more insulting and de-meaning than out-and-out prostitution. Moreover, in weighing and measuring the variables of Frenchwomen's liberty and equality, we found neither paradise nor purgatory but, rather, weaknesses and strengths in some areas, inequities and compensations in others, variety and complexity—and throughout the century an active, though not always astounding, participation of women in French social, political, economic and domestic life.

In the last analysis, what seems most important is not the quantity of freedom and equality, not the assessing and comparing of socio-economic gains and losses of the eighteenth-century female popula-tion of France, but the quality of the lives that these women led. Not what degree of prestige and power females had attained as a group, but how individual women of the age had enriched themselves and those around them. The fascination of eighteenth-century French-women is that so many among them expanded their horizons beyond their rococo pasteboard stage sets, understanding all the while that an intelligent and fulfilled woman can remain a feminine person of beauty and grace.

Style at the End of the Century (Boyer)

Notes

Notes To Chapter 1

1. *Lettres persanes,* Paris, Garnier, 1960, pp. 131–2.
2. Paris, Pagnerre, 1853, p. 126.
3. We have thoughtfully delayed her arrival until after 1723 and the crowning of Louis XV, since Louis and his successor were much more kindly disposed to the nobility than was the Regent Philippe d'Orléans.
4. This was Gardel, the dance master for the Opéra, for court ballets, and the Queen's dancing teacher.
5. Madame de Genlis, *Mémoires sur le 18e siècle et la révolution française.* Vol. I, Paris, Ladvocat, 1825, pp. 240–243.
6. *La Femme au 18e siècle,* Paris, Charpentier, 1877, p. 1.
7. *Ibid,* p. 6.
8. See Chapter 3.
9. A nun at the convent.
10. *Les Liaisons dangereuses,* Paris, Gallimard, 1952, pp. 26–27.
11. Madame d'Epinay, *Mémoires et correspondance,* Paris, Volland, 1818, Vol. I, p. 115.
12. *Ibid,* p. 110.
13. *Romanciers du 18e siècle,* Ed. Etiemble, Paris, Pléiade, 1965, Vol. II, p. 162.
14. *Ibid,* p. 163.
15. It is true, as we shall see in Chapter 4, that if her behavior became scandalously adulterous, legally her husband could have her confined to a convent. It happened, although less and less often.
16. Léon Abensour, *La Femme et le féminisme avant la révolution,* Paris, Leroux, 1923, p. 84.
17. *Op. cit.,* p. 224.
18. They won their freedom through money, pressure, riots or the initiative of their feudal lord.
19. Bader, Clarissa, *La Femme française dans les temps modernes,* Paris, Didier et Cie, 1883, p. 89.

20. Lacroix, Paul, *Le 18e siècle,* Paris, Firmin-Didot, 1875, pp. 72–73.
21. *Op. cit.,* p. 157.
22. *Op. cit.,* p. 255.
23. *Les Contemporaines,* Paris, Eds. du Trianon, 1930, Vol. II.
24. Paris, Garnier-Flammarion, 1965, p. 103.
25. Paris, Garnier, 1963, pp. 92–93.
26. *Op. cit.,* p. 95.
27. Quoted in Goncourt, pp. 244–245.
28. This does not take into account the prostitute, about whom we shall speak later.
29. A survey of 1790 showed that ten million out of twenty-three million French were in need of relief and that three million of these were paupers or beggars (Lefebvre, Georges, *The Coming of the French Revolution,* New York, Vintage, 1947, p. 95).
30. Abensour, p. 242.
31. See Jean-Jacques Rousseau's diatribe against the immorality of theatre artists in his famous *Letter to d'Alembert.*
32. Emile Campardon, *Madame de Pompadour et la cour de Louis XV,* Paris, Plon, 1867, pp. 79–81.
33. Paris, Garnier, 1964, p. 438.
34. *Op cit.,* p. 64.
35. Manon was, actually, a good cut above a common prostitute. She came undoubtedly from the *petite bourgeoisie,* took noblemen and wealthy farmers-general as lovers and, when her luck was with her, lived in the high style of a top-ranking courtesan.
36. *Op. cit.,* p. 104.
37. Goncourt, p. 292.
38. See Chapter 2 (Figaro's protest).
39. Memoirs, London, Harvill Press, 1969, p. 130.
40. *Op cit.,* p. 172.

Notes To Chapter 2

1. *Paradoxe sur les femmes, où l'on tâche de prouver qu'elles ne sont pas de l'espèce humaine,* Cracow, 1776.
2. *Controverse sur l'âme de la femme,* Amsterdam, 1744.
3. *La Femme n'est pas inférieure à l'homme,* London, 1750.
4. Article "Femme" in the *Encyclopédie* (1751–1772)

5. *Système social,* London, 1774, Vol. II.

6. *L'Ami des femmes ou philosophie du beau sexe,* Paris, 1758.

7. *Encyclopédie ou dictionnaire raisonné des sciences, des arts et des métiers,* Germany, Friedrich Frommann Verlag, 1967, Vol. VI, p. 469.

8. Amsterdam, 1753.

9. *L'Ami des femmes ou philosophie du beau sexe,* Paris, 1758.

10. *Essai sur le caractère et les moeurs des femmes d'après les différents siècles,* Paris, 1772.

11. Vol. VI, p. 472.

12. *Oeuvres,* Paris, Pléiade, 1951, p. 988.

13. *Ibid,* p. 981.

14. *Ibid,* p. 984.

15. He declared, "When you write about women, you should dip your pen in a rainbow and scatter dust from butterfly wings along the lines," *Ibid,* p. 986.

16. *Oeuvres complètes,* Paris, Pléiade, 1951 *(Esprit des lois),* Livre VI, Chap. III, p. 752. (Elsewhere in this work Montesquieu did recommend the right to repudiate husbands in those countries where a wife was her husband's slave.)

17. *Morale universelle,* Vol. I, Tours, Letourmy, 1792, p. 280.

18. *Op cit.,* p. 127.

19. *Théâtre,* Paris, Gallimard, 1966, Vol. I, p. 499.

20. *Théâtre,* Paris, Garnier-Flammarion, 1965, p. 202.

21. Puisieux's treatise is written as though by a woman but it is listed in the Bibliothèque Nationale under the name of the Marquis de Puisieux. Some critics have attributed it to his wife, but we shall assume that Monsieur is responsible for the document, since Madame de Puisieux's *Conseils à une amie,* Paris, 1749, in-12, is a much less daring work. For example, in educating females she would restrict the study of languages to princesses and have ordinary females learn to dance or walk gracefully instead. It should also be noted that Diderot was known to have contributed to Mme de Puisieux's writings when they were lovers, and that this work could conceivably have been composed by them while the two were "collaborating," between 1746 and 1751.

22. Actually Rousseau had little choice in the matter: infatuated with his beautiful employer, he had embarrassed Madame Dupin by dropping passionately to his knees before her. She was kind enough to forget the scene and keep him on as her secretary.

23. Fragments of the work passed from hand to hand and were finally sold

at the Drouot auction hall in Paris a few years ago. At this writing they are being readied for publication by Professor Leland Thielemann of the University of Texas. Michel Launay, in his *Jean-Jacques Rousseau et son temps,* Paris, Nizet, 1969, gives a résumé of some of the important points in Madame Dupin's notes.

24. *Les Gynographes,* La Haye, Paris, Eds. du Trianon, 1931, p. 92.

25. *Avis aux dames,* Paris, Bibl. Nat. L b 39, in-8, p. 604.

26. London and Paris, Royer.

27. *Très sérieuses remontrances des filles du Palais-Royal à messieurs les nobles,* Paris.

28. *Ibid,* p. 20.

29. *Procès-verbal et protestation de l'ordre le plus nombreux du royaume,* les c..., Paris, p. 1.

30. *Ibid,* p. 13.

31. *Ibid,* p. 12.

32. *Réponse des femmes de Paris à la protestation de l'ordre le plus nombreux de France,* Paris, 1789.

33. Abensour, pp. 450–451.

34. "Sur l'Admission des femmes au droit de cité," *Oeuvres* (3 Juillet, 1790), Paris, Didot Frères, 1847, Vol. X, p. 121.

35. *Emile,* Paris, Garnier, 1964, p. 446.

36. "Epître à Madame du Châtelet," (Preface to "Alzire") *Oeuvres complètes,* Paris, De l'Imprimerie de la Société Littéraire et Typographique, 1784, Vol. II, p. 365 (Nous sommes au temps, j'ose le dire, où il faut qu'un poète soit philosophe, et où une femme peut l'être hardiment.").

37. "Lettres à Monsieur de Voltaire sur la Nouvelle Héloïse" (1761).

38. "Epître CVI" (1769) *Oeuvres complètes,* Paris, Garnier, 1877, Vol. X, p. 409.

39. Letter to Francesco Albergati Capacelli, Sept. 12, 1764, *Correspondance,* ed. by Th. Besterman, Geneva, Institut et Musée Voltaire, 1960, Vol. 56, Letter 11243, p. 15.

40. *Op. cit.,* p. 494.

41. *Ibid.,* p. 502.

42. *Ibid.,* p. 540.

43. Paris, Garnier, 1960, p. 14.

44. *Ibid.,* p. 30.

45. *Ibid.,* p. 454.

46. *Op. cit.,* p. 517.

47. *Ibid.*

48. Op. cit., p. 203.

49. Paris, Garnier, 1964, p. 18.

50. *Ibid.*

51. The strong hand that Voltaire's niece, Madame Denis, eventually achieved does not contradict this pattern. If that avaricious woman took advantage of Voltaire, especially toward the end of his life, we can trace this exceptional situation to his blind indulgence toward her and his dependency on her in his old age, rather than any chronic need or desire for female domination.

52. *Op. cit.,* p. 453.

53. *Op. cit., p. 205.*

54. Correspondance, Letter to Monsieur Berger (October 18, 1736), Vol. V, Letter 1125, p. 279.

55. *Ibid.* (Dec. 1732) Vol. II, Letter 537, p. 412.

56. *Op. cit.,* p. 345.

57. *Oeuvres complètes,* Paris, Garnier, 1879, Vol. XXIV, p. 286.

58. "Zaïre," *Ibid,* Vol. II, p. 557.

59. "Ode sur les malheurs du temps (1713), *Ibid.,* Vol. II, p. 557.

60. *Discours sur les sciences et les arts,* Paris, 10/18, p. 230n.

61. *La Nouvelle Héloïse,* p. 68, "My father has sold me! He's made merchandise of his daughter, a slave!"

62. Abbé Galiani, *Correspondance,* Paris, E. Asse, 1771, Vol. I, pp. 203 ff.

63. Albert de Luppé, *Les Jeunes filles dans L'aristocratie et la bourgeoisie à la fin du 18e siècle,* Paris, Champion, 1924, p. 4.

64. *Tableau de Paris,* pp. 295–296.

65. (1783) *Oeuvres complètes,* Paris, Pléiade, 1943, p. 482.

Notes To Chapter 3

1. In Le Lyonnais, at the end of the seventeenth century, eight out of a hundred women could read and write; at the end of the eighteenth century, the number increased to sixteen per hundred. In Le Forez, the rate increased from ten to fifteen per hundred over the same period of time, and in Le Dauphiné, from nine to sixteen (Abensour, pp. 57–59). From 1686 to 1690, out of 217,009 marriage contracts, 29.6 percent of the men signed their names; 13.97 percent of the women signed theirs. From 1786 to 1790, out of 345,226 marriage contracts, 47.5 percent of the men signed their names; 26.87 percent of the women signed theirs (Edmée Charrier,

L'Evolution intellectuelle féminine, Paris, Albert Mechelinck, 1931, p. 30).

2. Paul Rousselot, *Histoire de l'Education des femmes en France,* Paris, Didier, 1883, Vol. I, p. 287.

3. *Ibid.,* p. 288.

4. *Essai Sur les femmes, Oeuvres,* Paris, Verdière, 1825, Vol. IV, p. 119.

5. Established in 1688, this school remained open after Madame de Maintenon's death in 1719, until just after the Revolution (1793).

6. Paris in 1765 had eight abbeys, seven priories and sixty-six convents.

7. In 1790, the small congregation of Notre-Dame housed thirty nuns and thirty to forty *pensionnaires;* in 1778, L'Abbaye-aux-Bois, the most highly populated convent, had 181 nuns (77 of them *dames religieuses;* 104, *soeurs converses),* 177 *pensionnaires,* eight novices, fifty-four administrators not to mention a large number of servants. Generally speaking, provincial convents were more populous than Parisian ones.

8. Seven to ten years old.

9. Supervisor of classes.

10. Albert de Luppé, *Les Jeunes filles,* pp. 79–80.

11. *Ibid.,* p. 62.

12. *Ibid.,* p. 86.

13. Luppé, *Une jeune fille au 18e siècle; Lettres de Geneviève de Malboissière,* Paris, Champion, 1925, (Letter of March, 1766), p. 141.

14. Rousselot, Vol. II, p. 97.

15. *Ibid.,* p. 116.

16. In these post-Freudian days, when many middle-class, enlightened parents worry about whether they are rejecting their children and giving them complexes, it is interesting to note that on the whole, ex-convent girls didn't appear to make more neurotic adults than home-bred ones (was there such a thing as a neurotic female before the romantic movement?) They were all in the same boat and considered living away from their families a natural state of affairs.

17. For an accurate account of this nun's (Marguerite Delamarre's) vain attempt to leave her convent, see Georges May, *Diderot et La Religieuse,* Paris, Presses Universitaires, 1954.

18. Luppé, *Lettres de Geneviève de Malboissière* (Letter of July, 1764 ("Alle trè e trè quarte del doppo pranzo), pp. 127–128.

19. (1746-1830).

20. By the time of the Revolution, all 100 Paris convents had these free day schools.

21. *Introduction à l'inventaire sommaire des archives départementales antérieures à* 1790, Versailles, Cerf, 1897. These were arguments advanced in order to counter a proposal for a free girls' school in Chevreuse. Although this particular case was disputed in 1650, arguments such as this one continued during the eighteenth century.

22. The date that Valmont de Bolmare started his celebrated public course in natural history.

23. *Rapport et projet de décret sur l'organisation générale de l'instruction publique,* in the name of the Committee of Public Instruction, 1792.

24. Roger Picard, *Les Salons littéraires et la société française, 1610-1789,* New York, Brentano's, 1943, p. 203.

Notes To Chapter 4

1. Voltaire made these satirical remarks about French laws in general: "We usually follow customary law because we know that a custom established by pure chance is always the wisest thing. Besides, customs, like clothes and coiffures, have all changed greatly in every province, so that judges can freely opt for a usage that was in vogue four centuries ago or one that was the rage last year. . . . All this means a sure fortune for practitioners, a good resource for shysters and a positive boon for judges who can, in all conscience, decide a case without understanding it" ("André Destouches à Siam," *Oeuvres complètes,* Société littéraire, 1784, Vol. XXXVI, p. 193).

2. Robert Pothier, *Traité de la puissance du mari sur la personne et les biens de la femme,* Paris, DeBure, 1770, Vol. I, p. 2.

3. *Op. cit.,* Vol. VI, p. 477.

4. *Traité du contrat de mariage,* Paris, Letellier, 1813, Vol. II, Part VI, p. 67.

5. In some provinces ruled by codified law, a bride sometimes entered marriage with "paraphernalia," private possessions or funds that would remain her very own, unsupervised by her mate; but in regions of customary law, any wealth or property that she possessed on entering marriage was considered her dowry. More realistically, it served as a source of investment in agricultural and commercial enterprises.

6. If a wife died, her husband received the *whole* of their property.

7. A number of marriage contracts contained the clause that a wife might later renounce the community arrangement and recover her original share plus any gifts or inheritances that she might have acquired through the years of her marriage. But usually the marriage contract specified

quite rigidly the respective portions that man and wife were to put into community property and did not allow for any subsequent changes or modifications on his or her part.

8. The Napoleonic Code endorsed these civil restrictions, and they remained in effect until the first years of the twentieth century.

9. *Op cit.,* p. 476.

10. According to Pothier, even minors (those under twenty-five years of age) could make contracts. Their guardians' assistance was needed only in the interests of the minors, whereas a wife needed her husband's authorization because the husband's power was "not established in favor of the wife but in favor of the husband" *(Traité des obligations,* Paris, DeBure Père, 1777).

11. In Roman times laws prohibiting married women from engaging in public life were aimed mainly at curbing the common male practice of using their wives' energies as political fuel for their own interests. A married couple could certainly wield influence more efficiently than a single male.

12. *Traité des obligations,* Vol. I, p. 4.

13. Pothier, *Traité du contrat de mariage,* Vol. II, pp. 84–85.

14. *Ibid.,* Vol. II, p. 94.

15. Sainte-Pélagie was undoubtedly not so comfortable as the convent where Madame de Stainville was confined. We read on occasion that it housed other personal maids of wayward ladies.

16. *Op. cit.,* Charpentier, pp. 241–242.

17. Even Protestant women in France were not allowed to divorce but were expected to conform to Church canons and the law of the realm. Interestingly enough, French Jews were considered a nation apart, so Jewesses were permitted to divorce, according to their own custom.

18. If they succeeded in marrying her off, they had no other legal obligations toward her. If, however, she still remained a spinster at twenty and the only sister in the family, she could demand a dowry worth up to one-third of the total inheritance, but if she had other unmarried sisters her share was less.

19. *Encyclopédie* (article "Tutrice"), Vol. XVI, p. 767.

20. *Ibid.*

21. Some writers have contended that the elegant hoop skirts of the day had been invented to disguise embarrassing pregnancies. According to Mercier, in the final stages of pregnancy, a Parisian bachelor girl could pretend to visit an aunt in the country, but could await her baby and have

it delivered in one of many private Paris houses run by discreet midwives.

22. Some of these women had brought their fief to marriage as their dowry; some shared in their husband's administration of feudal property; others were widows supervising their late husband's domain. They were not a rarity. In 1789 almost as many women as men held fiefs in the region of Le Quercy.

23. See Chapter 2.

24. See note 1. above.

25. *Op. cit.,* p. 116.

26. Paris, Garnier-Flammarion, 1965, p. 72.

Notes To Chapter 5

1. *Op. cit.,* p. 374.

2. Alexandre Samouillan, *La Société française au 18e siècle d'après les mémoires,* Paris, J. de Gigord, 1913, p. 124.

3. *La Nouvelle Héloïse,* p. 254.

4. Let us note that during this time, women, unlike men, were not allowed the experience of painting nude subjects. For examples of paintings by little-known French female artists, see *Les Femmes peintres au 18e siècle,* Castres, Musée Goya, 1973.

5. Where usually only men were invited, with the exception of Julie de Lespinasse.

6. Although some women did so unofficially. Paule-Marie Duhet reports, for example, that a few women, mainly soldiers' wives, did battle at the frontier *(Les Femmes et la révolution, 1789–1794,* Paris, Julliard, 1971, pp. 117–118).

7. *Ibid.,* p. 131.

8. *Ibid.,* p. 122.

9. Gita May, *De Jean-Jacques Rousseau à Madame Roland,* Geneva, Droz, 1964, p. 206.

10. *Women of the French Revolution,* Philadelphia, Henry Carey Baird, 1855, p. 38.

11. Duhet, p. 68.

12. 1792 was a big year for women's manifestos. In England that year Mary Wollstonecraft published her *Vindication of the Rights of Women.*

13. Simone de Beauvoir, *Le Deuxième sexe,* Paris, Gallimard, 1962, Vol I, p. 184.

14. Duhet, p. 155.

15. Alice Hurtrel, *La Femme, sa condition sociale depuis l'antiquité jusqu'à nos jours,* Paris, G. Hurtrel, 1887, p. 86.

16. *Op. cit.,* p. 115.

17. *Les Contemporaines,* Paris, Eds. du Trianon, 1930, p. 120.

18. But the Julie doll would continue to enchant the romantics.

Bibliography

Social Histories of Eighteenth-Century France

Barber, Elinor G., *The Bourgeoisie in Eighteenth-Century France,* Princeton, Princeton Univ. Press, 1955.

Lacroix, Paul, *Le Dix-huitième siècle, institutions, usages et costumes (France, 1700-1789),* Paris, Firmin-Didot, 1875.

Pernoud, Régine, *Histoire de la bourgeoisie en France,* 2 vols., Paris, Seuil, 1962.

Sée, Henri, *La France économique et sociale au dix-huitième siècle,* Paris, Colin, 1933.

Saint-Germain, Jacques, *La Vie quotidienne en France à la fin du grand siècle d'après les archives d'Argenson,* Paris, Hachette, 1965.

Works on the Eighteenth-Century Frenchwoman

Abensour, Léon, *La Femme et le féminisme avant la révolution,* Paris, Leroux, 1923.

Goncourt, Edmond et Jules de, *La Femme au dix-huitième siècle,* Paris, Charpentier, 1877.

Luppé, Albert, Comte de, *Les Jeunes filles dans l'aristocratie et la bourgeoisie à la fin du dix-huitième siècle,* Paris, Champion, 1924.

Social Histories of Frenchwomen (and Women in General)

Bader, Clarissa, *La Femme française dans les temps modernes,* Paris, Didier et Cie, 1883.

Decaux, Alain, *Histoires des françaises,* Vol II, "La Révolte," Paris, Librairie Académique Perrin, 1972.

Fagniez, Gustave, *La Femme et la société française dans la première moitié du dix-septième siècle,* Paris, J. Gamber, 1929.

Hurtrel, Alice, *La Femme, sa condition sociale,* Paris, Geo. Hurtrel, 1887.

Joran, Théodore, *Les Féministes avant le féminisme,* Paris, Gabriel Beauchesne et fils, 1935.

Lefèvre, Maurice, *La Femme à travers l'histoire,* Paris, Albert Fontemoing, 1902.

Lehmann, Andrée, *Le Rôle de la femme dans l'histoire de France au moyen âge,* Paris, eds. Berger-Levrault, 1952.

Reynier, Gustave, *La Femme au dix-septième siècle, ses ennemis et ses défenseurs,* Paris, Tallandier, 1929.

Memoirs, Correspondence and Chronicles

Mme du Châtelet, *Lettres,* publ. by Th. Besterman, Geneva, Institut et Musée Voltaire, 1958.

Mme d'Epinay, *Mémoires et correspondance,* Paris, Volland, 1818.

Mme de Genlis, *De l'Esprit des étiquettes de l'ancienne cour,* Rennes, Hyacinthe Caillière, 1885.

―――. *Mémoires sur le dix-huitième siècle et la révolution française,* Paris, Ladvocat, 1825.

Lespinasse, Julie Jeanne Eléonore de, *Correspondance avec le comte de Guibert,* ed. Villeneuve-Guibert, comte de, Paris, Calmann-Lévy, 1906.

Ligne, Prince de, *Mémoires et mélanges,* Paris, Ambroise Dupont, 1827.

Luppé, *Lettres de Geneviève de Malboissière à Adélaïde Méliand, (1761–1766),* Paris, Champion, 1924.

Mercier, Louis Sébastien, *Tableau de Paris,* Paris, Pagnerre, 1853.

Métra, *Correspondance secrète, politique et littéraire,* 2 vols., London, John Adamson, 1787.

Mme de la Tour du Pin, *Memoirs,* London, Harvill Press, 1969.

Voltaire, François-Marie Arouet de, *Correspondance,* ed. by Th. Besterman, Geneva, Institut et Musée Voltaire, 1960.

Feminist and Antifeminist Treatises of Eighteenth-Century France.

Avis aux dames, Paris, 1788 (Bibl. Nat. L b 39).

Boudier de Villemert, *L'Ami des femmes ou philosophie du beau sexe,* Paris, 1758.

Caffiaux, Père, *Défense du beau sexe,* 3 vols., Amsterdam, 1753.

Condorcet, Antoine-Nicolas Caritat, Marquis de, "Sur l'Admission des femmes au droit de cité," *Oeuvres,* Vol. X, Paris, Didot Frères, 1847.

Mme de Coicy, *Les Femmes comme il convient de les voir,* London and Paris, 1735.

Controverse sur l'âme de la femme, Amsterdam, 1744, mentioned in Beauvoir, Simone de, *Le Deuxième sexe,* Vol. I, Paris.

Mme de Gacon-Dufour, *Mémoire pour le sexe féminin contre le sexe masculin,* Paris and London, 1787.

Paradoxe sur les femmes, où l'on tâche de prouver qu'elles ne sont pas de l'espèce humaine, Cracow, 1776 (cited by Prof. Leonard M. Friedman, Chicago, MLA, 1971).

Poulain de la Barre, *De l'Egalité des deux sexes,* Paris, chez Jean du Puis, 1776.

Puisieux, Philippe-Florent, Marquis de, *La Femme n'est pas inférieure à l'homme,* London, 1750.

Mme de Puisieux, *Conseils à une amie,* Paris, 1749.

Procès-verbal et protestation de l'ordre le plus nombreux du royaume, les c. . . , Paris, 1789 (Bibl. Nat. L b 39, 1827).

Réponse des femmes de Paris à la protestation de l'ordre le plus nombreux de France, Paris, 1789 (Bibl. Nat. L b 39, 1828).

Restif de la Bretonne, *Les Gynographes,* La Haye, Paris, Eds. du Trianon, 1931.

Saint-Pierre, Abbé de, "Lettre à Mme Dupin sur les femmes," Villeneuve-Guibert, Gaston, *Le Portefeuille de Mme Dupin,* Paris, 1884.

Thomas, Antoine-Léonard, *Essai sur le caractère, les moeurs et l'esprit des femmes dans les différents siècles,* Vol. 4, Paris, Verdière, 1825.

Très sérieuses remontrances des filles du Palais-Royal à messieurs les nobles, Paris, 1788 (Bibl. Nat. L b 39 1073).

Pedagogical Works and Histories of Feminine Education

Mme de Campan, *De l'Education,* Paris, Maudouin Frères, 1824.

Chabaud, L., *Les Précurseurs du féminisme, Mesdames de Maintenon, de Genlis et Campan, leur rôle dans l'éducation chrétienne de la femme,* Paris, Plon, 1901.

Charrier, Edmée, *L'Evolution intellectuelle féminine,* Paris, Albert Mechelinck, 1931.

Fénelon, François de Salignac de la Mothe, *Education des filles,* Paris, E. Belin et fils, 1882.

Mme de Genlis, *Adèle et Théodore,* Paris, chez Maradan, 1804.

Rousselot, Paul, *Histoire de l'Education des femmes en France,* 2 vols., Paris, Didier, 1883.

Saint-Pierre, l'abbé de, *Un Projet pour perfectionner l'éducation,* Oeuvres, Vol. I., Paris, chez Briasson, 1778.

Pertinent Legal Texts

Beaune, Henri, *Droit coutumier français,* Paris, Delhomme et Briguet, ca. 1898.

Brissaud, Jean, *History of French Private Law,* Boston, Little Brown, 1912.

Colin, Ambroise et Capitant, Henri, *Cours élémentaire de droit civil français,* Paris, Librairie Dalloz, 1947.

Glendon, Mary Ann, "Matrimonial Property: A Comparative Study of Law and Social Change," *Tulane Law Review,* November, 1974.

Lacombe, Maurice, *Essai sur la coutume poitevine du mariage au début du dix-huitième siècle,* Paris, Champion, 1910.

Lefebvre, Charles, *Cours de doctorat sur l'histoire du droit matrimonial français,* Paris, J.-B. Sirey, 1908.

Pothier, Robert, *Traité du contrat de mariage,* Paris, Letellier, 1813.

———. *Traité des obligations,* Paris, DeBure Père, 1777.

———. *Traité de la puissance du mari sur la personne et les biens de la femme,* Paris, DeBure, 1770.

On Frenchwomen and the Revolution

Duhet, Paule-Marie, *Les Femmes et la révolution,* 1789–1794, Paris, Julliard, 1971.

Lefebvre, Georges, *The Coming of the French Revolution,* New York, Vintage, 1947.

Michelet, Jules, *Women of the French Revolution,* Philadelphia, Henry Carey Baird, 1855.

Villiers, baron Marc de, *Histoire des clubs de femmes et des légions d'amazones,* Paris, Plon, 1910.

Relevant Literary and Philosophical Works

Beaumarchais, Pierre-Augustin Caron de, *Théâtre,* Paris, Garnier-Flammarion, 1965.

Challes, Robert, *Les Illustres françoises,* 2 vols., Paris, Les Belles Lettres, 1959.

Diderot, Denis, *Oeuvres complètes,* Paris, Pléiade, 1943.

Encyclopédie ou dictionnaire raisonné des sciences, des arts et des métiers, Germany, Friedrich Frommann Verlag, 1967.

Holbach, Paul Heinrich Dietrich, Baron d', *Morale universelle,* Tours, Letourmy, 1792.

———. *Système social,* London, 1774.

Laclos, Choderlos de, *Les Liaisons dangereuses,* Paris, Gallimard, 1952.

Marivaux, Pierre Carlet de, *Le Paysan parvenu,* Paris, Garnier-Flammarion, 1965.

———. *Théâtre,* 2 vols., Paris, Gallimard, 1966.

———. *La Vie de Marianne,* Paris, Garnier, 1963.

Mercier, Louis Sébastien, *Tableau de Paris,* Paris, Pagnerre, 1853.

———. *Tableau de Paris,* 12 vols., Amsterdam, 1782–1789.

Prévost, Antoine-François, Abbé de, *Manon Lescaut,* Paris, Garnier, 1962.

Restif de la Bretonne, *Les Contemporaines,* Paris, Eds. du Trianon, 1930.

———. *Le Pornographe,* Brussels, Gay et Doucé, 1879.

Rousseau, Jean-Jacques, *Les Confessions,* Paris, Garnier, 1964.

———, *Les Discours, Le Contrat social,* Paris, Le Monde en 10/18, 1963.

———. *Emile,* Paris, Garnier, 1964.

———. *Lettre à d'Alembert sur les spectacles,* Paris, Garnier-Flammarion, 1967.

———. *La Nouvelle Héloïse,* Paris, Garnier, 1960.

Montesquieu, Charles Louis de Secondat, Baron de la Brède et de, *Les Lettres persanes,* Paris, Garnier, 1960.

———. *Oeuvres complètes,* Paris, Pléiade, 1951.

Romanciers du Dix-huitième siècle, 2 vols., Paris, Pléiade, 1965.

Voltaire, François-Marie Arouet de, *Oeuvres complètes,* Paris, Société Littéraire et Typographique, 1784 and Ed. Moland, Paris, Garnier, 1877.

Selected Works on Eighteenth-Century Frenchwomen

Campardon, Emile, *Madame de Pompadour et la cour de Louis XV,* Paris, Plon, 1867.

Goncourt, Jules and Edmond, *Sophie Arnould,* Paris, Flammarion, s.d.

Herold, J. Christopher, *Love in Five Temperaments,* (Mmes Tencin, Aïssé, Staël, Lespinasse, Clairon), N. Y., Atheneum, 1961.

May, Gita, *De Jean-Jacques Rousseau à Madame Roland,* Geneva, Droz, 1964.

Ségur, Pierre, Marquis de, *Julie de Lespinasse*, N. Y., E. P. Dutton, 1927.

Wade, Ira Owen, *Studies on Voltaire with some Unpublished Papers of Madame du Châtelet*, Princeton, Princeton Univ. Press, 1947.

Villeneuve-Guibert, Gaston, Le Portefeuille de Mme Dupin, Paris, 1884.

Miscellaneous

Beauvoir, Simone de, *Le Deuxième sexe*, 2 vols., Paris, Gallimard, 1949.

Fauchery, Pierre, *La Destinée Féminine dans le roman européen du 18e siècle*, (1713-1807), Paris, Colin, 1972.

Les Femmes peintres au 18e siècle, Castres, Musée Goya, 1973 (exposition brochure distributed by Worldwide Books, Boston).

Introduction à l'inventaire sommaire des archives départementales antérieures à 1790, Versailles, Cerf, 1897.

Launay, Michel, *Jean-Jacques Rousseau et son temps*, Paris, Nizet, 1969.

May, Georges, *Diderot et la Religieuse*, Paris, Presses Universitaires, 1954.

Michelet, Jules, *La Femme*, Paris, Hachette, 1873.

Picard, Roger, *Les Salons littéraires et la société française 1610-1789*, New York, Brentano's, 1943.

Clandestine Love (Le Prince)